DISCOVERING ART SERIES

17th & 18th Century Art

adapted by Ariane Ruskin

Foreword by Howard Conant
New York University

McGRAW-HILL BOOK COMPANY

New York • San Francisco • Toronto

Also in the Discovering Art Series:

NINETEENTH CENTURY ART adapted by Ariane Ruskin
CHINESE & ORIENTAL ART adapted by Michael Batterberry
TWENTIETH CENTURY ART by Michael Batterberry

Acknowledgment is hereby given to Purnell & Sons, Ltd., for the right to base this work on the text of the magazine series "Discovering Art" and to Fratelli Fabbri Editori for the right to make adaptations from the Italian text of *Capolavori Nei Secoli.*

17th & 18th CENTURY ART
Illustrations copyright © 1961–1964, 1969 by Fratelli Fabbri Editori, Milan, Italy. No part of this work may be reproduced without the permission of the publisher.

All Rights Reserved. *Printed in Italy.*

Library of Congress Catalog Card Number: 69-17190

FOREWORD

by Howard Conant, *Professor and Chairman, Department of Art Education; and Head, Division of Creative Arts, New York University*

IN THIS volume Ariane Ruskin has meticulously recorded and traced every significant influence upon and aspect of a great era in European art—the seventeenth and eighteenth centuries. Beyond her scholarly approach as an art historian, however, she brings the valuable gift of a fine literary style to her work, for *17th & 18th Century Art,* as adapted by Miss Ruskin, has the interesting and readable prose one usually associates with a first-rate, carefully researched historical novel. Its narrative moves along in a way that is compelling and exciting, as well as logical and soundly based on fact. Thus, in a way, it becomes in itself a work of art. Its colorful and vivid background and narrative flow are an apt expression of the eventful history and the superb art it records.

It is particularly appropriate that Miss Ruskin's exceptional talents and her knowledge have now been applied to the arts of these centuries. It is a period that has been treated by many with disdain, perhaps because, subjectively, they equate the art too closely with the historical situation or mistakenly categorize all of it as frivolous and superficial—in the process, ignoring some of the unique and greatest artistic personalities of the time. Still others may have turned away from the arts of this period because they are unable or unwilling to relate the great accomplishments of the baroque and the rococo to functional modern living.

Once again, however, the superb, richly embellished arts of seventeenth- and eighteenth-century Europe are being looked upon with favor. Elaborate costume and extravagant styles, modish grooming, intricate patterning, sundry *objets d'art,* and the splendors of baroque music—all long thought to be irrelevant, overly flamboyant, and sugary—have survived the workings of historical cycles in taste and are again being appreciated and emulated. Even conservative adults are gradually introducing bright color and ornate design into their wardrobes and into the "functional" or cautiously traditional interiors they have long lived with. This marked change in public taste is, in large measure, due to the artistic interests and creative expressions of the younger generation. With the freshness and natural casualness of youth and with obvious relish, they have decidedly thrown off the shackles of the sober "functionalism" long imposed by machine culture and industrial design, with its sometimes antiseptic and inhuman results.

Like other volumes in the "Discovering Art Series," *17th & 18th Century Art* is not a dull, superficial "survey course" treatment of its subject. Created for use by a general (and primarily youthful) audience, it is a text that is ideally suited for a wide-ranging and, at the same time, probing examination of the society and cultural contributions of a specific period. Invaluable for use in this sort of "humanities" context, it also makes a handsome and very useful addition to the home library of the general reader.

CONTENTS

INTRODUCTION

DURING THE seventeenth and eighteenth centuries, all of Europe was gradually introduced to, and came to grips with, the art of the Italian Renaissance. It is true that the Low Countries (present-day Netherlands and Belgium) had already enjoyed a splendid rebirth of art that was more or less independent of Italy. It is true, too, that Germany had already seen the work of Albrecht Dürer (1471–1528) and Hans Holbein the Younger (1497/8–1543), and Spain the marvels of El Greco (1541–1614). But these men were individual and revolutionary figures, and both Dürer and El Greco had studied in Italy. It was not until the seventeenth century, in fact, that the art of the Italian Renaissance became of truly international currency. Yet in each country where it took root, it was so deeply imbued with the national character of the people and influenced by their political and religious institutions that the various art styles differ strongly, and these differences are visible at a glance. *The Massacre of the Innocents* (Plate 1-1) by the Italian Guido Reni (1575–1642) and *The Meeting of the Officers of the Militia Company of St. Hadrian in Haarlem* (Plate 1-2) by the Dutch painter Frans Hals (1500/85–1666) are the product not only of different schools of art but of very different cultures.

At the turn of the seventeenth century, Europe was in a period of ferment. Outside Italy much of the Continent was still emerging from the confusion of feudal strife and the rash of religious wars connected with the Protestant Reformation. Separate nations with firm national characters and governments centralized in the power of a national monarch took the place, once and for all, of the constantly warring nobility of the Middle Ages; and England, Spain, and France attained much the same national confines we recognize on the map today. In the first decade of the seventeenth century, France was ruled by the "Good King," Henry IV, who patched up the wounds of religious conflict and prepared the way for the prosperous rule of the "Sun King," his grandson Louis XIV. In England, the Elizabethan period was coming to a close, and the island kingdom basked in its newly achieved naval power and enjoyed the literary "renaissance" of the Shakespearean age. Both countries were well on their way toward brilliant futures.

Germany was still divided into many small states, however, and was soon to suffer the cruel impoverishment of the Thirty Years' War. In Spain the descendants of the insane daughter of Ferdinand and Isabella, Juana the Mad, all of her line apparently being somewhat deranged, held the Iberian peninsula in the grip of a powerful, stifling, and despotic autocracy, largely financed by gold and silver from the New World. By virtue of its Hapsburg king, Philip II, Spain controlled the Netherlands, which was struggling for its freedom.

Thus, the political scene varied from country to country, and about 1600 Italy was the most politically disrupted—though still artistically the most brilliant—of all the Western European lands.

1-1. *The Massacre of the Innocents,* by Guido Reni

As mentioned above, the various international art styles took on distinct cultural traits in the different European nations; and the political situation and level of national consciousness varied from country to country in this epoch. Within countries, also, there were clear differences in the emphasis or importance given the various arts, and in their degree of stylistic development.

Italy, as well as France perhaps, might be said to have produced a more "even" distribution of first-rank achievements among all the arts than did the other Western European nations considered here. On the whole, most countries seem to have excelled in specific arts at any one time or, for instance, to have had a flourishing baroque style in certain arts but not in others, or never to have practiced the fully developed rococo style that one finds in France and Austria. For varied motives, in areas such as the Low Countries baroque and rococo architecture, for example, never reached the florid heights and elaborate scale attained in the Latin lands and, especially, in Aus-

tria and Bavaria. In these last-named regions, painting and sculpture were noteworthy mainly for what they contributed to the decorative arts and to the architectural ensemble. The independent panel painting did not have a notable history in the Germanic territories during these centuries, whereas this same period encompassed some of the greatest accomplishments in Dutch painting, which had been preceded by the Flemish marvels of Rubens. Rembrandt and, in Spain, Velázquez had no true peers in the other arts among their countrymen.

Once he is aware of such substantial differences in political, cultural (particularly religious), and artistic circumstance, the reader should then understand the reasons for the varying emphasis—both according to region and among the individual arts—necessary in any general study such as this. Within this complex panorama, however, the seventeenth and eighteenth centuries can be said to mark off one of the great eras in Western European art.

1-2. *Meeting of the Officers of the Militia Company of St. Hadrian in Haarlem* (detail), by Frans Hals

Italy

ITALY in the seventeenth century was, like Germany, a "geographical expression"—a land area consisting of many small independent states, republics, and kingdoms, each of which was an entity in itself. There was no effective political unity, no overriding national consciousness. An inhabitant of Turin would have been conscious of being Piedmontese but would have had no idea of belonging to an Italian national state.

Moreover, with no one of her small states able to match the terrifying force of the Northern European monarchies, Italy became during the fifteenth century the battleground for the two most powerful rulers of the time, Francis I of France and the Hapsburg emperor Charles V, who held the kingdoms of Naples, Sicily, and Sardinia as part of his Spanish empire and wished to be the dominant force in the entire Italian peninsula. He succeeded in winning a series of devastating wars, which were fought mostly by mercenaries and which resulted in the sack of Rome in 1527 and the final fall of the Florentine republic. Charles V was crowned both Holy Roman Emperor and King of Italy by the Pope in 1530, and by the middle of the century he had allied himself with and dominated entirely a group of Italian ruling houses, many of them united to him by ties of marriage: the Sforzas in Milan, the Gonzagas in Mantua, the Estes in Ferrara and Modena, and the Medicis in Florence. Venice was an independent city, and papal Rome a separate state. The largest part of Italy remained under Spanish control for the entire seventeenth century, but it was a land impoverished by war and taxation and suffering under the heavy hand of the Inquisition, the church tribunal, more Span-ish than Italian in character, which curbed expression of all thought not felt to be in keeping with church doctrine.

In his book *The Italians,* Luigi Barzini describes the piteous political state of Italy under Spanish domination:

> Society appeared formed of two main layers. At the top were a few *grands seigneurs.* At the bottom the vast ragged, picturesque and powerless crowds. The *grands seigneurs* derived their power mostly from the favors of the king and from the revenue of their land. They were encouraged to live lavishly, on their estates or at court, and not to dabble in trade, banking, politics, or scholarly pursuits. Cosimo I de' Medici, to avoid trouble, forced the great banking and trading families of Florence to invest their capital in country estates and rewarded them with sonorous titles. Titles were much sought after. The nobility cut off from responsibilities inevitably became overbearing, inept and dull. The populace was kept ignorant, poor, superstitious, harassed by tax-collectors, religious authorities, bureaucrats and soldiers. At times the poor broke out in bloody but short-lived and unprofitable riots. Most of the time, they were kept happy in their misery by the distribution of alms, the sale of cheap flour, the splendid performance of public spectacles and the clubs of policemen. The show was all important. This is why the Baroque age is still unsurpassed in the breath-taking beauty of public buildings, churches, parks, residences and cities. It was not an accident that all great architects of the day were also famous scenic designers. Historical events were, whenever possible, staged like sumptuous theatrical productions.[1]

Art, then, was far from dead in Italy. And the particularly theatrical style in all the visual arts that came to be known as "baroque" may have been, in a way, the Italians' reaction to and escape from the tedium and oppression they found about them. The baroque style that developed in

[1] Luigi Barzini, *The Italians,* Atheneum Publishers, New York, 1964.

the seventeenth century was also well suited to the religious fervor of the Catholic Counter Reformation, the passionately pious reaction to the Protestantism that had caused so many countries of northern Europe to break away from the Church of Rome.

What, then, was "baroque"? It was a style that was extremely ornate and decorative. The word itself probably stems from the Portuguese *barroco* or the Spanish *barrueco,* meaning an irregularly shaped pearl. In later centuries when the strict, clean lines of classical art were again preferred, the word was used as a term of criticism; but today baroque art has come to be accepted as a significant epoch in art history, notwithstanding the fact that some critics consider its flights of fancy to be too exuberant. The painters, sculptors, and architects of seventeenth-century Italy could look back upon the immense body of Renaissance art which they saw in every church and at every street crossing. They very naturally sought to take the best of what former generations had to offer, but they also wanted to surpass what had gone before. Like the English writers of the period, who Lyly's Euphues said[2] wanted to create "better poetry than could be made of words," the baroque sculptors, painters, and architects wanted to create better works of art than could be made of paint and marble. Baroque art was born in Italy, but it soon became an international style.

Among the earliest painters important in the baroque movement was Michelangelo Merisi (1573–1610), called Caravaggio for his birthplace near Milan. In the brief span of his tumultuous life he created canvas after canvas in the manner which eventually became associated with baroque painting and which was frequently copied in the century

[2] John Lyly, *Euphues, or the Anatomy of Wit,* 1578.

following his death. He did everything possible to create a sense of drama and strong emotion in his works. In paintings such as his *Madonna of Loreto* (Plate 1-3), showing the Christ Child held in the arms of his mother and worshiped by awed pilgrims, and in his painting *The Flagellation of Christ* (Plate 1-4), the scenes are presented in a prevailing darkness dramatically illuminated by brilliant spots of light, and the figures are depicted in powerfully twisted poses. In keeping with the tastes of his day, Caravaggio painted morbid visions of ghastly events, such as his *Beheading of St. John the Baptist* or *David with the Head of Goliath* (Plates 1-5, 1-6), once again scenes of darkness that are bathed in an eerie light. And yet he was known, too, for the brightly colorful, decorative charm of many of his works, particularly those painted earlier in his career—for example, his picture entitled *The Gypsy Fortuneteller* (Plate 1-7), a painting

1-3. *Madonna of Loreto* (detail), by Caravaggio

1-4. *The Flagellation of Christ,* by Caravaggio

1-5. *The Beheading of St. John the Baptist,* by Caravaggio

1-6. *David with the Head of Goliath,* by Caravaggio

of a palm reader gazing into the hand of a jauntily dressed cavalier. These extraordinary effects of light and darkness were achieved by the then rarely used method of painting shadows over lighter areas rather than highlighting darker ones.

The superbly painted glass, fruit, and leaves of his *Bacchus* (Plate 1-8) remind us that Caravaggio was among the first Italian painters interested in still life; a small basket of fruit he painted early in his career was perhaps the first Italian painting that might be considered a deliberate still life, that is, an arrangement of objects in a picture which includes no human subject. Like most of the masters of the baroque period, Caravaggio was expert at painting convincing textures of cloth and flesh.

And yet, for all that Caravaggio's religious paintings, such as his *Rest on the Flight into Egypt* (Plate 1-9), were deeply moving, no artist of his time was more violently criti-

15

cized, especially by the clergy. The Italian-born Spanish painter Vicencio Carducho (1576–1638) said of Caravaggio, "I heard a zealot of our profession say that the appearance of this man [Caravaggio] meant a foreboding of ruin and an end of painting, and how at the end of this visible world the Antichrist, pretending to be the real Christ, with false and strange miracles and monstrous deeds would carry with him to damnation a very large number of people moved by his [the Antichrist's] works which seemed so admirable. . . ."[3] Strangely enough, the cause of this scathing criticism was Caravaggio's *realism.* The painter frequently set episodes from Christ's life in the most ordinary of surroundings, totally with-

out magnificent historical trappings. On occasion, entire scenes, such as *The Calling of St. Matthew* (Plate 1-10), were interpreted in the fashion of Caravaggio's own day. This had been done before, but never with such telling detail. The sweaty-looking tormentors in *The Flagellation of Christ* (Plate 1-4) are dressed in grubby jerkins and shirts, in disarray from their violent activity. It was said in reproach that the pilgrims in his *Madonna of Loreto* (Plate 1-3) were dirty and that he had used the cadaver of a strumpet drowned in the Tiber as model for his *Death of the Virgin* (Plate 1-11).

These accusations may have had some substance, for in his private life Caravaggio would seem to have been less than exemplary. He was described as being a very dark man with peculiar habits. It was said that "he adorned himself with velvet and

[3] Elizabeth G. Holt (ed.), *A Documentary History of Art,* Vol. II, Doubleday & Company, Inc., 1958, p. 209.

1-7. *The Gypsy Fortuneteller,* by Caravaggio

other fine materials, but when he had put on one costume, he never changed it until it had fallen into rags. He was very negligent of personal cleanliness and for many years, morning and evening, he used the canvas of a portrait as a tablecloth." According to his biographer, the rival painter Giovanni Baglione (1571–1644), Caravaggio "was a satirical and haughty man; he would often speak badly of all painters of the past and present, no matter how distinguished they were, because he thought that his works surpassed all the other men of his profession." Noted for his fearful temper, he was constantly in trouble with the police. As a result of his personal failings, he came to a questionable end. In the words of Baglione,

> Because of the excessive ardour of his spirit, Michelangelo [Caravaggio] was a little dissolute and sometimes he seemed to look for the occasion to break his neck or even risk the lives of others . . . in the end he got into a fight with Ranuccio Tomassoni, a very likeable young man. Because of certain differences over a game of ball they challenged one another to a duel and came to arms. Michelangelo gave Ranuccio a thrust which sent him to the ground with a wounded thigh and killed him. Everyone involved in the affair fled from Rome. . . . Afterwards he went to Malta [where] he had a dispute with a certain Cavaliere di Giustizia and somehow insulted him. For this he was thrown into prison, but escaped at night by means of a rope ladder and fled to the island of Sicily. In Palermo he executed several works, but because he was still being pursued by his enemy he had to return to Naples. There his enemy finally caught up with him and he was so severely slashed in the face that he was almost unrecognisable.[4]

On his way back to Rome and a pardon, Caravaggio stopped off at Porto Ercole, and

[4] Giovanni Baglione, *Le vite de' pittori, scultori ed architetti* ("Lives of the Painters, Sculptors and Architects"), Rome, 1642.

1-8. *Bacchus,* by Caravaggio

here his final misfortune befell him. He was mistakenly imprisoned for two days and, upon his release, learned that the boat he thought to be carrying his possessions had already sailed. In sheer rage he started along the beach in the July sun in the hope of catching sight of it, was seized with a fever, and died a few days later. His effects were in fact being held in the local customs shed.

Despite the official rejection of many of his works by some of the clergy, Caravaggio had many patrons and imitators. The disapproving Carducho said,

> His new dish is cooked with such condiments, with so much flavor, appetite and relish he has surpassed everybody with such choice tid-bits and a license so great that I am afraid the others will suffer apoplexy in their true principles, because most painters follow him as if they were

famished. They do not stop to reflect on the fire of his talent, which is so forceful, nor whether they are able to digest such an impetuous, unheard of and incompatible technique, nor whether they possess Caravaggio's nimbleness of painting without preparation.[5]

Carducho's fears were well founded, and the works of Caravaggio's closest followers and imitators appear far weaker than the powerful compositions of the master himself. Outstanding among these were Orazio Gentileschi (1563–1638), who emigrated to England to become court painter to Charles I, and his daughter Artemisia (c. 1597–after 1651), one of the few female painters of the era. Although technically excellent, Gentileschi's *David* (Plate 1-12) appears ineffectual when placed beside Caravaggio's tense and active portrayal of the same subject. In the same artist's painting of the third-century martyrs Cecilia, her betrothed Valerian, and his brother Tiburtius (Plate 1-13), the figures seem weightless and artificially posed in their seventeenth-century dress. His daughter's Caravaggesque style was typified in religious subjects such as *Judith with the Head of Holofernes* (Plate 1-14).

More to the taste of the period were the works of the Carraccis and their school. There were three Carraccis, Lodovico (1555–1619) and his cousins, the brothers Agostino (1557–1602) and Annibale (1560–1609) Carracci, who banded together, about 1585/1586, to found a teaching academy in Bologna known as the "Accademia degli Incamminati" (academy of "those set on the right road"). This was to become the most famous school of its kind, the training ground for many of the most celebrated Italian painters of the next generation. The aim of the academy was not to develop a revolutionary new technique but

1-9. *Rest on the Flight into Egypt* (detail), by Caravaggio

to return to the strength, harmony, and directness of the finest days of the Renaissance. A roughly translated sonnet by Agostino Carracci sums up their views:

Whoever a goodly painter seeks to be
Should take the Romans' drawing to his aid,
Movement from the Venetians, and their shade,
And worthy coloring from Lombardy,
The awesome Michelangelo must see,
The truth to nature Titian has displayed,
The pure and sovereign style Correggio had,
And of a Raphael just symmetry,
Tibaldi's basis, and his decoration,
Invention of learned Primaticcio's own,
And just a little grace from Parmigianino. . . .[6]

If the baroque painters of the Carraccis' Bolognese academy departed from these traditions, it was not deliberately but because the spirit of their time was so very different from that of previous centuries. They seemed in a way to try to replace the simple religious faith of former periods with ex-

[5] Holt, *op. cit.*, p. 209.

[6] *Ibid.*, pp. 73–74.

1-10. *The Calling of St. Matthew,* by Caravaggio

1-11. *The Death of the Virgin* (detail), by Caravaggio

travagant and sometimes exaggerated fervor (Plate 1-15).

Many of the works of the Carraccis and their followers, such as *The Madonna and Child Enthroned* by Lodovico Carracci (Plate 1-16), show the baroque style in a well-developed state. As in the works of Caravaggio, figures are portrayed in twisted poses and in deeply shadowed settings. There is dramatic lighting, but from an elusive source, and the fluttering drapery is caught up in a mysterious wind. Baroque paintings often expressed strong emotions and were meant to arouse them in the viewer—be it a feeling of fear or of awe, as in the case of the *Madonna and Child.* Lodovico worked mainly in Bologna and stayed on to conduct the academy after both his cousins had left for Rome. By doing so (and this was his greatest achievement), he was able to raise Bologna to the level of a vital center of art for all of Italy.

1-12. *David,* by Orazio Gentileschi

1-14. *Judith with the Head of Holofernes*, by Artemisia Gentileschi

1-13. *The Martyrs Valerian, Tiburtius, and Cecilia,* by Orazio Gentileschi

1-15. *The Communion of St. Jerome,* by Agostino Carracci

1-16. *Madonna and Child Enthroned,*
by Lodovico Carracci

1-17. *The Madonna of the Rosary* (detail),
by Lodovico Carracci

Lodovico was a slow and diligent worker, by some compared unfavorably with his cousins. Certainly toward the end of his life his work suffered a decline, perhaps because he felt overshadowed by Annibale's talent and renown in Rome. However, Lodovico collaborated successfully with his cousins in decorating the houses of the nobility during their early years in Bologna. There is also much beauty, charm, and grave piety in the work that is distinctly his own. He was very highly regarded by English artists in the eighteenth century. Sir Joshua Reynolds, who recommended him as a model, declared that he approached perfection in his power over his materials. In paintings such as Lodovico's *Madonna of the Rosary* (Plate 1-17), the lighting is particularly dramatic: the Madonna is darkly outlined against a brilliantly lit background, while the infant St. Francis falls under a ray of bright illumination. A recognizable characteristic of Lodovico's work is the treatment of the hands of all his figures; elongated and sensitive, they convey a feeling of great tenderness.

Unquestionably the greatest of the Carraccis was Annibale, whose career took him to various places in Italy, and eventually to Rome. Annibale, who can be seen in his extraordinary *Portrait of the Artist with His Father and Nephew Antonio* (Plate 1-18), came closest to the spirit of the High Renaissance that all three of the Carraccis sought. He was capable of portraying violent action, as in his *Stoning of Saint Stephen* (Plate 1-19); yet many of his compositions, such as *The Flight into Egypt* and *Christ and the Woman of Samaria at the Well* (Plates 1-20, 1-21), have the peaceful grandeur, the warm light, and the soft color associated with works painted a century earlier. Still, even in these we can see two extraordinary characteristics of baroque painting: the tiny figures in the

1-18. *Portrait of the Artist with His Father and Nephew Antonio,* by Annibale Carracci

1-19. *The Stoning of St. Stephen,* by Annibale Carracci

background which seem only casually suggested by a few strokes of the brush and which are much smaller than those in the foreground, although they do not appear to be at a great distance, so that it would seem that the rules of scientific perspective have been broken. This was frequently done by baroque artists, who, though they hoped to recapture the art of the High Renaissance, were only too willing to break its rules for dramatic effect.

Annibale was seriously interested in landscape for its own sake. In his painting *The Sacrifice of Isaac* (Plate 1-22), the group of figures, with the angel staying Abraham's arm as he is about to strike his son, is almost incidental to the picture, which is in fact a tremendously "romantic" and distinctly Italian landscape that in no way evokes the biblical setting of the Holy Land. Finally,

Annibale's amazing versatility can be seen in works such as *The Bean Eater* (Plate 1-23), depicting a peasant with grimy fingernails hungrily attacking a dinner of beans, bread, and chives, with an earthenware jug of wine at his elbow. More "realistic" than anything painted by Caravaggio, Annibale's treatment is more permissible since it is not a sacred subject.

The Academy of the Carraccis in Bologna produced several of the finest painters of the next generation, including Guido Reni (1575–1642); Domenico Zampieri (1581–1641), known as "Domenichino" (meaning "Little Dominic"); and Guercino (1591–1666).

Reni's *Massacre of the Innocents* (Plate 1-1), portraying Herod's wholesale killing of the infants in the hope of slaying the Messiah, is an excellent example of the baroque artist's love of painting figures poised in the midst of violent action. Most Renaissance masters had shown a preference for stable, balanced, and orderly compositions that were serene in effect; but to the painters of the baroque period, individual figures were less important than the overall effect of a design full of movement and rhythm. Baroque painters and sculptors came to realize that a powerful sense of change, the suggestion of a balance which is threatened, arouses the emotions because it plays on the nerves. They used this expressive discovery to the full, and examples are legion. In one of his altarpieces, Caravaggio creates immense tension by showing a stool about to topple from a platform. The baroque artist's desire to stir the emotions profoundly resulted in a change in subject matter. More fervid religious sentiments and subjects such as the martyrdom of saints were much commoner in the seventeenth century than they had

1-20. *The Flight into Egypt* (detail), by Annibale Carracci

1-21. *Christ and the Woman of Samaria at the Well,* by Annibale Carracci

1-22. *The Sacrifice of Isaac,* by Annibale Carracci

ever been before. Profound religious experiences, with their sense of heightened emotion, and scenes of gruesome death expressed far better than a tranquil company of saints the baroque period's preference for art that produced a powerful response.

Reni's *Massacre of the Innocents* was regarded as particularly fine because the whole range of emotions was considered suitable: the executioners of the children must be brutal; the mothers pathetic and helpless, showing in their anguished faces the purity of their souls. It was held that each emotion must be given a corresponding external expression. If the emotion was extreme, the gestures must be suitably dramatic. Thus, expressions and gestures that may seem exaggerated to us today were created in all seriousness and were deeply felt.

In the eighteenth century Guido Reni was regarded as one of the very greatest of European artists, though today he is not so highly considered. In Charles Kingsley's novel *Alton Locke* (1849), a character is so moved by Reni's *St. Sebastian* that he exclaims, "Great tears, I know not why, rolled slowly down my face." Oddly enough, it was just about this time that Reni's reputation began to suffer a decline. One of the reasons for this was the mid-nineteenth century's "discovery" of early Italian art, compared with which Reni's work seemed exaggerated and insincere—which it was not. Nonetheless, a century after he lived, the Empress Catherine of Russia, greedy for works of art, is said to have paid £3,500 for Reni's *Immaculate Conception*, an enormous sum for that time, when works by as great a master as Rembrandt could be had for as little as £300. But it is not hard to imagine how a painting such as Reni's *The Baptism of Christ* (Plate 1-24), viewed

1-23. *The Bean Eater,* by Annibale Carracci

1-24. *The Baptism of Christ,* by Guido Reni

1-25. *Atalanta and Hippomenes* (detail),
by Guido Reni

1-27. *The Martyrdom of St. Peter* (detail), by Domenichino

1-26. *Portrait of the Artist's Mother,*
by Guido Reni

in its original setting over an altar in a darkened church, with its forms seen by flickering candlelight, might exert a compelling spell.

Like most artists of the period, Reni portrayed scenes from the classical mythology of Greece and Rome as well as from the Bible: for example, his painting of the race between the huntress Atalanta and her suitor Hippomenes (Plate 1-25). He was admired for his painting of nude and draped figures which suggested classical Greek or Roman statues but which were filled with the violent and dramatic motion of the baroque. Still, like Caravaggio and Annibale Carracci, he was interested in realism and direct observation of nature. This can be seen in his sensitive portrait of his mother (Plate 1-26).

Domenichino's *Martyrdom of St. Peter* (Plate 1-27) bears comparison with Reni's *Massacre of the Innocents*. Both are scenes of the same kind of violent action, and both are based on designs from the masters of the High Renaissance. Reni's was influenced by a composition by Raphael, and Domenichino's group of St. Peter and his slayer was adapted from a painting by Titian of the same subject destroyed by a fire in the nineteenth century. If we note that the murderer on the left in Reni's painting is a much more recognizable individual than St. Peter's slayer, we begin to perceive the reason for Reni's particular excellence.

Like Annibale Carracci, but unlike Reni, Domenichino was interested in landscape, which became more and more important during this period, although still frequently enhanced by small figures. These views, painted not from nature but from the imagination, were often meant to suggest the calm, comforting countryside of the shepherd heroes of the classical writings of Theocritus or Vergil, and are therefore

1-28. *Landscape with Hercules and Achelous* (detail), by Domenichino

known as "pastoral" landscapes. In Domenichino's *Landscape with Hercules and Achelous* (whom Hercules slays in the form of a white bull), the inclusion of this episode from Greek mythology adds to the learned quality of the painting (Plate 1-28), which art patrons well-versed in the classical myths and legends would have appreciated.

Of the three most famous students of the Carraccis, Guercino began most brilliantly. He was something of a child prodigy. Born Giovanni Francesco Barbieri in Cento, a small town near Bologna, he came to be known as Guercino, or "squint-eyed," because of a sight defect that he had since childhood. In his painting of Susanna espied at her bath by the Elders (Plate 1-29), the Elders are painted with a Caravaggio-like realism, whereas Susanna is a figure of ideal beauty inspired by classical statuary. The use of flickering light aids in the effect of a just arrested motion, and the whole scene is bathed in a mysterious, shadowy atmosphere. It is a sad fact that later in life Guercino's style became cold and uninteresting and that he produced rather lifeless

1-29. *Susanna and the Elders,* by Guercino

1-30. *Death of Cleopatra,* by Guercino

pictures, such as his *Death of Cleopatra* (Plate 1-30), with the Egyptian queen wanly clutching the poison asp to her breast—a pretty figure flatly painted and without character.

Although trained in Bologna, Agostino and Annibale Carracci, Guido Reni, Domenichino, and Guercino eventually all went to Rome. With a thorough training in the painting of large-scale frescoes (a technique perfected during the Renaissance whereby pigments were applied to wet plaster into which they seeped and were fixed), these artists could expect, and in fact received, important commissions from rich and powerful patrons. Rome was, in the seventeenth century, the unquestioned capital of art, and it was here that the baroque style was first fully developed and found its greatest expression. There are several reasons for this—the most important being the Council of Trent (1545–1563), which laid down that art could, and should, be used for the propagation of religion. Moreover, because it was felt that Rome herself should visibly reflect her position as the center of the Christian world, there arose a desire to create a new and more impressive city. Successive popes, beginning with Sixtus V, therefore set themselves to remodeling it.

The opportunities these projects gave to painters, sculptors, and architects of the era were immense. Commissions were plentiful, and thus the city attracted artists from far and wide. This constant influx of new talent meant that art in the papal capital was in a perpetual state of renewal, expansion, and change. With the turn of the seventeenth century, the important new forces of Caravaggio and the Carraccis appeared on the Roman scene.

Then, from the 1620's until his death in 1680 there was, above all, Gian Lorenzo Bernini (1598–1680). The greatest master of the Italian baroque, Bernini was recognized as such in his own time. He was immensely successful, and his talents were varied: he was a designer of fountains (the movement of rushing water was much appreciated in the baroque period and fountains became popular) and responsible for their popularity, a creator of theatrical décor, a caricaturist, and a writer of comedies. Preeminently, of course, he was a sculptor, painter, and architect. And never before had architecture, painting, and sculpture been more closely united, melting into each other to create one vast illusion. Baroque architects, like baroque painters,

1-31. Sant' Andrea al Quirinale, Rome, by Gian Lorenzo Bernini

1-32. *The Triumph of St. Ignatius,* by Andrea Pozzo

broke all the loosely held rules of their trade to achieve dramatic emotional effect. During the Renaissance classical architecture, borrowed from the Romans, was substantially altered, but certain of the antique rules were retained in a calm and restrained manner: columns stood on bases, capitals on columns, and arches or horizontal entablatures on capitals, and surfaces were usually flat and rectangular. But in the churches and other structures of the baroque period, nothing is so classically stable and calm. Walls recede and advance; surfaces are convex and concave; the classical orders, the prescribed forms of base, column, capital, and entablature, were treated in new ways and flamboyantly curved architectural details were added. Like a baroque painting, the facade of a baroque building kept the eye in motion. Bernini's Sant' Andrea al Quirinale in Rome (Plate 1-31) is a small but perfect example of this style in church architecture.

1-33. *The Ecstasy of St. Theresa,* by Gian Lorenzo Bernini

1-34. *The Death of the Blessed Lodovica Albertoni,* by Gian Lorenzo Bernini

In the interior of buildings baroque artists combined painting, sculpture, and architectural details to create a vast and elaborate illusion that would excite the emotions. The viewer cannot tell what is painted, what is sculpted, or what is an architectural element of such buildings. Often what appears to be sculpted decoration or architectural detail is simply illusionistic painting on the flat surface of a wall. Paint is made to look like marble, and marble is worked like cloth. In *The Triumph of St. Ignatius* (Plate 1-32), painted on the ceiling of the nave of the Church of Sant' Ignazio, Andrea Pozzo (1642–1709) succeeded in making the actual architecture of the church appear to extend into the heavens, where an allegorical scene representing the missionary zeal of the Jesuits is depicted. The perspective scheme works only if the spectator stands at a single spot, halfway down the nave, that is marked on the floor of the church. If he does, he feels himself wafted heavenward, and made slightly uneasy by certain figures that appear actually to be falling from the sky.

There was no more brilliant creator of illusion than Bernini. In the Cornaro Chapel of the Church of Santa Maria della Vittoria in Rome, he combined sculpture, architecture, painting, and natural light to re-create the exact moment of the ecstatic revelation of St. Theresa, the sixteenth-century Spanish reformer of the Carmelite order (Plate 1-33). The saint is seen, sculpted in seemingly weightless marble, floating toward heaven in a ray of light that is both sculptural and real, while an angel pierces her breast with a burning arrow. The artist depicted a moment of which the saint herself had had a mystic vision, which she described in her writings.

Bernini emphasized the emotional state of his sculpted figures by the use of fluttering or magnificently rumpled drapery, as in the

1-35. *David,* by Gian Lorenzo Bernini

funerary figure entitled *The Death of the Blessed Lodovica Albertoni* (Plate 1-34). In marble he created ridges of highlight and hollows of shadow that underline, by means of the agitated movement of the viewer's eye, the inner feelings of his subjects.

Like the painters of the period, Bernini tried to capture in his sculpture—the one art form he favored above all others—figures in the midst of an action that is often violent. His *David* (Plate 1-35) is seen as he is about to launch a stone from his slingshot, and the viewer is made to feel that there is an invisible Goliath just beyond the youth's shoulder. As in the case of the plummeting figures on Pozzo's ceiling, the spectator becomes involved in the action. Bernini's figure of Apollo is seen in the act of grasping Daphne, who, to escape him, at that very moment is turning into a laurel tree (Plate 1-36). In his bust of Costanza Buonarelli, the model is caught in the act of speaking (Plate 1-37).

Born in Naples, the son of an unexceptional sculptor and painter, Bernini rose in his lifetime to a position of great eminence. He was regarded as a child wonder, and his education was personally supervised by Pope Paul V. He was the principal architect for embellishing the interior of St. Peter's, and in 1665 he was invited to the court of Louis XIV, where he submitted designs for a section of the Palace of the Louvre. It was there that the Sieur de Chantelou, whom Colbert had appointed to accompany the artist, recorded Bernini's appearance and views on art. To the French Academy, Bernini stated a firm belief that students should study the classical works of Greece and Rome to achieve ideal, perfect beauty, free of any fault of nature. That Bernini trained himself in this manner is clearly evident. Both his *David* and the form of Apollo in his *Apollo and Daphne* are based on classical models. Thus, study of the great works of antiquity and also of the masters of the Renaissance, rather than of nature itself, became the set and stifling pattern of instruction for the day, especially in Italy.

There were a great number of other artists in Rome during the seventeenth century who should not be forgotten, notwithstanding Bernini's overpowering brilliance. One of the most moving sculptural works of the period was the *St. Cecilia* (Plate 1-38) by Stefano Maderno (1576–1636), who worked in the early part of the century. According to tradition, the figure represents the exact position of the body of the martyred saint (said to have suffocated in her bath) as it was found. [The tradition though is incorrect: she was beheaded.] During his lifetime, Bernini's only important rival as a sculptor was Alessandro Algardi (1595–1654), whose portrait of Pope Innocent X (Plate 1-39), the counterpart of Bernini's own statue of Pope Urban VIII

1-36. *Apollo and Daphne,* by Gian Lorenzo Bernini

in St. Peter's (Plate 1-40), shows a Bernini-like use of dramatic drapery—although Algardi himself was in general more representative of the academic classicism of the Bologna school.

Nor was Bernini the only unquestioned master of architecture. His almost exact contemporary Francesco Borromini (1599–1667) carried baroque architecture to the very limits of its brilliance and virtuosity. Borromini, an unbalanced eccentric who eventually committed suicide, was perhaps the most highly original architect of his time. The Church of Sant' Ivo (Plate 1-41), constructed in Rome between 1642 and 1660, is considered one of his greatest individual works. Here, on a six-pointed star-shaped plan, he executed a superb church roofed by a lanternlike structure that is surmounted by a sort of spiral ramp culminating in a Cross. Nothing could be further from the stable, balanced symmetry of classical or Renaissance architecture. Equally amazing was his facade for the

1-37. *Costanza Buonarelli,* by Gian Lorenzo Bernini

Church of San Carlo alle Quattro Fontane (Plate 1-42). The middle portion of the lower half of the design is convex in form, but the section immediately above is concave, and the whole is surmounted by an oval ornament. This free use of the curve, frowned upon by strict followers of classical architecture, led to an effect of movement.

Nor were Bernini and Borromini alone in the field of Roman baroque architecture. The genius of Pietro Berrettini, known as Pietro da Cortona (1596–1669), can be seen in the great curving portico he designed for the facade of the Church of Santa Maria della Pace (Plate 1-43). Cortona was a talented painter, and his knowledge of both painting and architecture enabled him to create lavish decorative ensembles, in which painting is offset by elaborately sculpted stucco flowers, garlands of leaves and fruit, cornucopias, trophies, cherubs, and such. At times these were executed in white against gold, and sometimes in gold on white or some other solid color. Moreover, in its color and detail, Cortona's painting was the richest and most luxuriant of the period, as can be seen in his portrayal of *The Age of Silver* (Plate 1-44), part of his decorations in the Pitti Palace in Florence depicting the Four Ages of Man. Cortona's elaborate taste in allegorical and legendary cycles (Plate 1-45) influenced palace decorations for generations.

Meanwhile, there were artists of talent outside Rome as well. In Florence, no longer a leading center of art, there were such painters as Baldassare Franceschini, called "Il Volterrano" (1611–1689), whose picture entitled *The Practical Joke of the Priest Arlotto* (Plate 1-46) is an excellent example of what is called "genre" painting—usually charming and sometimes sentimental depictions of everyday life. Naples claimed the very promising Bernardo Cavallino (1616–1656), who unfortunately died along

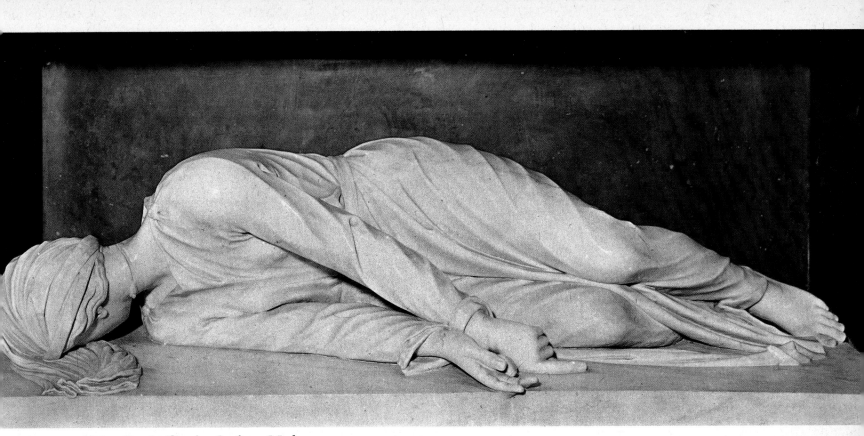

1-38. *St. Cecilia,* by Stefano Maderno

1-39. *Pope Innocent X,*
by Alessandro Algardi

1-40. Tomb of Pope Urban VIII,
by Gian Lorenzo Bernini

1-41. Sant' Ivo, Rome, by Francesco Borromini

with two-thirds of the population of the city in the terrible plague of 1656 and, therefore, left few canvases (Plate 1-47). Naples was also the home of some distinguished still-life artists, such as Giovan Battista Ruoppolo (1629–1693; Plate 1-48), and the most successful of Italian landscape painters, Salvator Rosa (1615–1673). Rosa, an extraordinary figure who acted, composed music, and wrote poems and satires (one such, directed against Bernini, led to Rosa's exile from Rome), was a favorite of eighteenth- and nineteenth-century art connoisseurs, who firmly believed him to have been a dashing bandit, because of the subject matter of his paintings. In any case, although Rosa lived two centuries before the romantic movement, the English essayist William Hazlitt proclaimed him to be "beyond question the most Romantic of landscape painters." Scenes like his *St. John the Baptist in the Wilderness* (Plate 1-49) conjure up a dramatic mood by means of a wild, rocky setting, the interplay of jagged branches and turbulent sky, and the acid coloring, all rather in the manner of "grand opera."

Milan, under the influence of Archbishop Charles Borromeo (later canonized) and his nephew Cardinal Federico Borromeo, produced painters of strong religious inspiration, among them Giovanni Battista Crespi, called "Il Cerano" (c. 1575–1632; Plate 1-50). Meanwhile, in wealthy Genoa, lavish palaces were covered with splendid frescoes such as the allegory of *Summer* (Plate 1-51) by Gregorio de' Ferrari (1647–1726), painted on a ceiling of the Palazzo Rosso.

Venice remained free of Spanish control in the seventeenth century; but, menaced by Spain nonetheless, and fighting a losing war against the Turks and with declining trade, she went into both political and artistic eclipse. Only in architecture did there continue to be real achievement. Un-

1-42. San Carlo alle Quattro Fontane, Rome, by Francesco Borromini

questionably the greatest of Venetian seventeenth-century architects was Baldassare Longhena (1598–1682), whose Church of Santa Maria della Salute (Plate 1-52) on the Grand Canal forms the central feature of one of the most stunning vistas in the whole of Italy. It was begun in 1631, in fulfillment of a decision made by the Venetian republic during the plague year of 1630 to erect a church as an offering. Its romantic domes and curling volute buttresses sum up the stage-set quality of Venetian baroque.

The few painters of note in Venice in this period were foreigners living in the Venetian republic, such as the German Johann Liss (c. 1595/97–1629/30; Plate 1-53). The schools of the great Venetian masters of the sixteenth century—Titian,

1-43. Santa Maria della Pace, Rome, remodeled by Pietro da Cortona

Tintoretto, Veronese, and Bassano—continued to function but produced little work worthy of mention. It is strange, then, that during the eighteenth century the palm for greatness in art was to pass from Rome to Venice.

After the death of the last Hapsburg king of Spain and the culmination of the Franco-Spanish wars with the Peace of Utrecht (1713), control of much of the territory of Italy passed from Spain to the Austrian Hapsburgs. The country, still divided into many small states in most regions, was in greater decay than ever; chaos and confusion reigned. There were 13,000 homicides in the Papal States alone during one ten-year period, and in Naples there were ten existing codes of law, and legal cases virtually centuries old. During most of this era the clergy and the aristocracy paid no taxes at all, and a prominent Neopolitan wrote, "If we divide all the families in the kingdom into sixty parts, one of these owns land, and fifty-nine have not sufficient to be buried in." And still there was a new stream of travelers from abroad. With the social and economic growth of the eighteenth century in northern Europe, there developed a species of humankind that had scarcely existed since the days of ancient Rome—the tourist.

Rome remained the center of tourist attention, and it was included in the itinerary of every English traveler's "Grand Tour."[7] Rome was admired not only for its Renaissance and baroque wonders but also for the ruins of antiquity, which were gradually being disclosed everywhere in the city as interest in archaeological diggings developed. Rome was still the capital to which students of art flocked, and without casting aside the powerful influence of the

[7] The traditional trip through the European continent, which usually followed a route from the British Isles through France, and often Germany, south into Italy.

1-44. *The Age of Silver* (detail),
by Pietro da Cortona

1-45. *The Story of Aeneas* (detail),
by Pietro da Cortona

Renaissance masters, they gradually fell more and more under the spell of ancient statuary and the crumbling remnants of ancient architecture. This interest was to have a profound influence on European art in the late eighteenth and the early nineteenth century, when the German Johann Joachim Winckelmann (1717–1768), the most important art historian of his time, published his monumental study of ancient art.

But it was not in Rome, nor anywhere in Italy, that the fashion in artistic style was now set. Under the intelligent guidance of Louis XIV in the previous century, France had become politically the greatest power in Europe—and through the endeavors of the king, his court, and ministers, the greatest cultural center as well. During the seventeenth and eighteenth centuries artistic taste was formed at Versailles, the seat of the court of Louis XIV and his successors

1-46. *The Practical Joke of the Priest Arlotto*, by Il Volterrano

to the throne, and for the most part was accepted throughout Europe. It was in France, then, that the reigning style of much of the eighteenth century—the rococo (the name may come from the French word *rocaille*, a kind of rock decoration)—was devised. Rococo was basically a style of interior decoration and architecture but, as the general taste changed, became a style in painting and sculpture as well. Very likely in reaction to the dramatic grandeur of the baroque, rococo emphasized all that was delicate and "pretty": finely curved moldings and softly hazy pictures in shades of pink, blue, mauve, and gold. It was a style given also to grotesquerie and fantasies, like monkeys in human dress, and was often influenced by the exquisite patterns painted on chinaware, which was then reaching Europe in large quantities.

Moreover, the spirit of rococo was always capricious and gay. Serious, dramatic, or deeply religious subject matter was deliberately avoided by rococo painters, as something altogether unsuited to the style. It is for this reason, perhaps, that rococo was never popular in Rome or Italy as a whole.

But Venice had become, by the eighteenth century, the most frivolous city in Europe, and it was Venice that produced several of the greatest rococo painters, and perhaps the most accomplished painter of the entire eighteenth century, namely, Giovanni Battista Tiepolo (1696–1770). As a secular power, Venice was in a condition of decadence. The great state that, almost alone,

had been powerful enough to challenge the papacy had declined into a tourist center. Though the Venetian republic still maintained its ambassadors at the courts of Europe, it had begun to neglect its mainland territories, gradually contracting until the state and city of Venice were one and the same in extent. Under a reactionary government, petty laws and regulations abounded. The city that had once been the center of European book production now suffered under repressive censorship. Poverty and corruption were rife. The principal public activities were processions and ceremonies, boating, and gambling. Montesquieu, that leading figure of the French Enlightenment, said: "My eyes are very pleased with Venice; my heart and mind are not."

Life in eighteenth-century Venice was minutely described by the many visitors who stopped there to admire its wonderous beauty and enjoy its pleasures. The Piazza San Marco (St. Mark's Square), then as now

1-48. *Still Life with Fruit,*
by Giovan Battista Ruoppolo

1-49. *St. John the Baptist in the Wilderness,* by Salvator Rosa

the heart of the city, was a scene of continuous activity, even turmoil. People of every nationality and rank were to be found there. Street vendors, beggars, fortunetellers, tightrope walkers, quacks, and musicians all mingled with citizens going about their everyday business, courtesans and cavaliers, or aristocrats passing through with their retinues. Along the quays, fishmongers spread their wares under colorful awnings.

The famed carnival of Venice, which traditionally began on December 26, gave occasion for a prolonged round of gaiety, highlighted by the celebrated masked balls.

1-50. *St. Michael Overcoming the Spirits of Evil,* by Il Cerano

1-51. *Summer* (detail), by Gregorio de' Ferrari

The mask, seen repeatedly in paintings of the Venetians, was an indispensable part of Venetian life. It was the great social equalizer by which its wearer could gain access into places normally reserved for patricians. Generally, it was made of black velvet or white waxed silk and designed to cover the upper half of the face. Worn with it, by men and women alike, was the *bautta,* a hooded mantle usually topped by a three-cornered black hat. Grotesque masks covering the whole of the face were worn only with fancy dress. Apart from carnival time, masking was permitted throughout the period of various public holidays.

It was for this strange and pleasure-loving city, then, that Tiepolo created his magnificent decorations. Tiepolo found his inspiration partly in the works of the great Venetian painter of the sixteenth century, Paolo Veronese, but he was also influenced, in both his use of color and his manner of interpreting historical and mythological episodes, by two outstanding Venetian painters of the generation just preceding his own, namely, Sebastiano Ricci (1659–1734) and the younger Giovanni Battista Piazzetta (1683–1754). Ricci, like Tiepolo later, spent a good deal of his time working outside Venice and traveled as far as London in search of commissions. His fresco of Hercules slaying the legendary monster Cacus (Plate 1-54) gives some idea of his grandly lit and sensitively colored decorations. Ricci's mature style was so close to that of Veronese that he was once accused of forgery, and at least one of his compositions was published in engraved form as a Veronese. Piazzetta, who also worked abroad, was held in such high repute that, upon the founding of the Venetian Academy in 1750 (one of many such learned societies involved with the arts that were then being established all over Europe), he was

1-52. Santa Maria della Salute, Venice, by Baldassare Longhena

chosen its first director. In his painting *Rebecca at the Well* (Plate 1-55), he shows the Venetian tendency to interpret biblical scenes in the gorgeous and worldly dress of the Venetian Renaissance. Here Rebecca is offered jewels by Abraham's curiously aristocratic servant, superbly fitted in Venetian dress, and the muzzle of a camel seen behind him is used to suggest an Oriental setting.

Tiepolo himself, though he studied with an obscure master, was precocious and received recognition early. In his twenties he was employed by the Venetian state, both as an artist and as curator of art treasures. Tiepolo's early works, exemplified by his paintings *The Angel Appearing to Hagar and Ishmael* (the wife and child whom Abraham had put aside; Plate 1-56) and *Abraham and the Three Angels* (Plate 1-57) are often cramped compositions and recall the more

1-53. *The Game of Mora,*
by Johann Liss

somber color of Piazzetta. But from early paintings like this, lit with a dramatic light that cast deep shadows, Tiepolo moved into a world of spaciousness and light in which his figures, like actors costumed by Veronese, danced rather than walked.

Having scored a great success with a series of frescoes on the life of Abraham for the Archbishop of Udine, Tiepolo strode across much of Europe—or rather, through that part in which the Catholic church and monarchies were still in absolute control. He never worked in London or Paris or, more surprisingly, in Rome. This phase of his career culminated in the astonishing triumph of the Anthony and Cleopatra frescoes for the ballroom of the Labia Palace in Venice. The work was created, with the aid of assistants, between 1745 and 1750. Two scenes from the story of Anthony and Cleopatra, *The Meeting* (Plate 1-58) and *The Banquet,* during which Cleopatra dazzled Anthony by her extravagance, are presented on facing walls, each set as if behind a screen of painted illusionistic architecture that surrounds and is hardly distinguishable from the real doors and windows which pierce the walls. In true baroque style, these real doors and windows seem to give access to the illusionary world of the fresco, but each central scene appears more immediately accessible by a short flight of painted steps leading directly from the ballroom floor. This vision of Egyptian antiquity is essentially theatrical and unreal. The architecture throughout is that of the Italian Renaissance. Cleopatra herself, surrounded by attendants and musicians, is dressed in the style of a sixteenth-century Venetian noblewoman. Tiepolo's genius in creating so dazzling an atmosphere can be pinpointed in the way that he suggested Cleopatra's retinue in the harbor with the device of no more than a cluster of faces.

Tiepolo's *Rinaldo Infatuated by Armida* (Plate 1-59) was painted three years later.

1-54. *Hercules and Cacus,* by Sebastiano Ricci

1-55. *Rebecca at the Well,* by Giovanni Battista Piazzetta

1-56. *The Angel Appearing to Hagar and Ishmael,* by Giovanni Battista Tiepolo

The legendary love between these two characters is mentioned in Torquato Tasso's epic poem "Gerusalemme Liberata" (Jerusalem Delivered). Rinaldo, leader of the First Crusade, was said to have fallen in love with Armida, a queen endowed with supernatural powers. Eventually Rinaldo was called away to fight, and Armida, in despair, set her palace afire and disappeared into thin air. As the last great master in the manner of the Italian Renaissance, at a time when the old ideals and beliefs that had sustained the artists before him were being questioned, Tiepolo used every painterly skill to materialize, to sweep the spectator into the center of his dream, where all men are gods for as long as they remain, and where time and mortality are suspended or held in abeyance.

Tiepolo's sketch of *Olympus* (Plate 1-60), the mountain home of the Greek gods, shows his late style—increasingly airy, with the color as luminescent as ever and the figures placed unerringly in the vast heavenly expanse. Yet the scene is more dreamily

1-57. *Abraham and the Three Angels,* by Giovanni Battista Tiepolo

portrayed than ever. The gods gaze detachedly, unaware of Hermes spiraling down with the aimless progress of an autumn leaf. The mellow light has a sunset glow.

The two sons of Tiepolo, Domenico (1727–1804) and Lorenzo (1736–1776), frequently assisted in his later projects. It is interesting to study Domenico's work in the decorations for the guesthouse of the Valmarana Villa, outside Vicenza, which he created while his father painted the walls of the villa itself. These are meant to be genre scenes of peasant life; yet Domenico's peasants are not real, but are romantically beautiful and elegantly turned idealizations who stroll in an imaginary setting. In his *Summer Stroll* (Plate 1-61), the parasols and fans, the misty landscape, all these details contribute to a sense of heat, and the women's full skirts and tiny feet give the

1-58. *The Meeting of Anthony and Cleopatra,* by Giovanni Battista Tiepolo

1-59. *Rinaldo Infatuated by Armida,* by Giovanni Battista Tiepolo

figures an extraordinary, rather theatrical charm. Domenico's paintings of clowns (Plates 1-62, 1-63), executed originally for the walls of his father's villa at Zianigo, sum up much of the spirit of Venice in this era. In the guise of Pulcinella (Punch), the stock character of Venetian comedy, a figure traditionally dressed in white, with large nose, large stomach, hunchback, and squawky voice, they lounge or cavort drunkenly.

At the same time, Venice did not lack portraitists. One of these, surprisingly, was a woman, Rosalba Carriera (1675–1757), who at the height of her career enjoyed a reputation that only her personal lack of beauty in any way diminished. In her later self-portraits (Plate 1-64), she frequently portrayed herself with her brow wreathed in laurel, as the tragic Muse. Meanwhile, genre paintings of scenes from the life of this extraordinary city and its environs were charmingly painted by Pietro Longhi (1702–1785; Plates 1-65, 1-66).

1-60. *Olympus,* by Giovanni Battista Tiepolo

1-61. *The Summer Stroll,* by Domenico Tiepolo

But apart from the great works of Tiepolo, Venice is best known for the *vedute,* her "views." This more humble form (as it was then considered) of landscape art became extremely popular, though not with the Venetians themselves. Tourists, especially the English, were eager to return from their Grand Tours with some tangible memento. A painting of Venice, the contemporary equivalent of the picture postcard, was essential. From this commercial traffic in art, despised by the Venetian Academy,

1-62. *Clowns Swinging,*
by Domenico Tiepolo

came two such *vedutiste* of great ability who are now highly regarded: Giovanni Antonio Canal, called "Canaletto" (1697–1768), and Francesco Guardi (1712–1793).

Canaletto was not the first of the Venetian view painters, but he was certainly the greatest. He came of a family of artists and began his career, as Ricci had, as a scene painter. Working for the theater was unsatisfying, and he soon turned to the example of his only important predecessor in this formal type, and possibly his teacher, Luca Carlevaris (1665–1731). Carlevaris had specialized in painting Venetian festivals, the great occasions of pageantry with which the declining Venetian state attempted to convince herself and her visitors that she remained a power in the world. These scenes were necessarily detailed and accurate. Canaletto included the characteristic detail, without always being absolutely truthful— that is, with more artistic selectivity.

1-64. *Self-portrait,* by Rosalba Carriera

1-63. *Clowns at Rest,* by Domenico Tiepolo

In his early works, those which won him his reputation, Canaletto achieved a meticulous accuracy of detail without sacrificing qualities of light and color that were worthy of the greatest older masters (Plate 1-67). Unfortunately, he lapsed into a kind of assembly-line production, assisted by pupils, in which methodically traced outlines on canvas were almost mechanically filled in with flat areas of color. Working mainly for English tourists, his reputation in England soared, but when he at last ventured across the Channel to that country, his technique—by then perfunctory—applied to familiar English scenes so disappointed his patrons that it was even rumored he was but an imposter.

In scenes such as his *View of the Dolo* or *Campo SS. Giovanni e Paolo* (Plates 1-68, 1-69), Canaletto meets the challenge of a complex perspective. In both these works the eye is led on a dizzying path across surfaces often foreshortened and seen from

1-65. *The Quack,* by Pietro Longhi

1-66. *Wild Duck Hunting in the Estuary,* by Pietro Longhi

many angles, in sunlight and in shade, with the result that the spectator is pulled directly into the picture. His two views of the Basin of St. Mark's—one seen close at hand (Plate 1-70), and the other from the Church of San Giorgio Maggiore (Plate 1-71)—give one a clear idea of the topography of the fascinating city. The Basin (or harbor) of St. Mark's was the focus of Venetian activity. For this reason it was not only painted repeatedly by Canaletto himself, but it also remained a challenge to every artist who visited Venice thereafter. The former, close-up view shows the Campanile (bell tower) on the left, the great open piazza (square) with the columns of St. Mark and St. Theodore, and the fourteenth-century Doge's Palace bordering on the water. The famous Bridge of Sighs is on the right. This entire view occupies only the extreme right segment of the San Giorgio Maggiore version, on the left side of which may be seen the dome of Santa Maria della Salute. The entire panorama is painted in the most minute detail; yet Canaletto has maintained a firm hold over the design of the entire marvelously airy composition.

Francesco Guardi and his older brother, Giovanni Antonio (1698–1760), who attracted little attention during their lifetime, are now as—or even more—highly thought of as are their more immediately successful

1-67. *View of the Grand Canal* (detail), by Canaletto

1-68. *View of the Dolo*, by Canaletto

contemporaries. Their impression on the public of their day was so slight, however, that very little of consequence is known of their lives, except that in 1719 their sister was married to Giovanni Battista Tiepolo. Until Giovanni Antonio's death, the brothers appear to have conducted a small workshop, producing whatever was demanded of them in their struggle in a highly competitive market. The Guardis' father also had been a painter, and their younger brother Niccolò was a member of the workshop as well, but Giovanni Antonio appears to have dominated his brothers and to have had ambitions as a history painter.

The Guardis' paintings of *Tobias Catching the Fish* (with which he was to cure his father's blindness) and *Tobias and His Wife in Prayer* (Plates 1-72, 1-73), panels created to decorate an organ for the Church of the Angelo Raffaele, give some idea of their style. Their manner was too gay in color,

1-69. *Campo SS. Giovanni e Paolo*, by Canaletto

1-70. *The Basin of St. Mark's,* by Canaletto

too insubstantial in form, and too light-weight in effect to create the serious impact suitable to historical or religious painting, but their work was saved from the rather coy prettiness that mars so much lesser baroque and rococo art by the sheer incandescence of their touch. And it was precisely in this virtuoso manipulation of paint that the originality of the Guardis lay. Applied with a delicate flickering brush, featherlike touches of luminous silvery color dissolve their often-borrowed forms (from the designs of other artists), creating a world of light-drenched mists and wraithlike figures. Flesh, fabrics, fur, feathers, and foliage all merge to become one variegated, shimmering stuff—a world spun in thistledown.

The Guardis were perhaps somewhat indebted for this extraordinary and original technique to the works of an oddly prophetic romantic Genoese painter, Alessandro Magnasco (1667–1749). Magnasco's dark pictures, illuminated by feverish brushstrokes of light color that are like flashes of lightning in the night, are charged with a strange

1-71. *The Basin of St. Mark's from San Giorgio Maggiore,* by Canaletto

1-72. *Tobias and His Wife in Prayer*, by Giovanni Antonio or Francesco Guardi

1-73. *Tobias Catching the Fish*, by Giovanni Antonio or Francesco Guardi

1-74. *Amusements in a Garden in Albaro* (detail), by Alessandro Magnasco

1-75. *The Parlor,* by Giovanni Antonio or Francesco Guardi

foreboding. His favorite subjects were ruined monasteries, synagogues, and scenes of witchcraft and satanic rites not unlike the disturbing visions of Goya's *pinturas negras* ("black paintings"). Even in his painting entitled *Amusements in a Garden in Albaro* (Plate 1-74), a scene of festivities in a park, his figures have an enigmatic and mysterious air. They seem to suggest an oncoming storm or some impending doom, rather than the light atmosphere of a summer picnic. Magnasco gave to his finished paintings the fresh spontaneity previously associated only with preparatory studies, and it was this direct and lightly sketched technique that most influenced the Guardis.

The Guardis, however, were quite capable of a "tighter" technique for subjects that required detailed treatment, like their genre painting of the parlor of a convent (Plate 1-75). To preserve the family holdings as well as possible, a great many children of the nobility in eighteenth-century Italy found themselves destined for religious vocations. The daughter of such a family would take with her all the privileges and favors of her rank. Visitors and admirers might be received in the convent parlor. The nuns behind the grille would dispense refreshments while entertainment, including concerts, balls, plays, or even puppet shows took place in the outer area of the parlor.

After the death of his brother Giovanni Antonio in 1760, Francesco turned increasingly to view painting, at first in direct emulation of Canaletto and probably in search of the latter's financial success. This popular commercial appeal, however, he never achieved; his prices were about one percent of those commanded by Canaletto,

1-76. *St. Mark's Square,* by Francesco Guardi

1-77. *The Island of San Giorgio,* by Francesco Guardi

though Guardi, too, eventually became a member of the Venetian Academy. Many of his pictures were exceedingly small, truly picture-postcard size. Unable to match Canaletto's microscopic accuracy of detail, he abandoned precision altogether; instead he created visions of space and twilight, which reflected the desolation of his native city, decaying among the lagoons (Plate 1-77).

Guardi's painting *St. Mark's Square* (Plate 1-76) is both literally and in spirit the reverse of Canaletto's paintings of the Basin of St. Mark's. It looks out across the harbor, with the Doge's Palace on the left and the base of the Campanile on the right. Canaletto emphasized the realities of the scene, carefully defining every visible detail of the architecture, and used light and shade to create that magical clarity with which the eye is dazzled on a sunlit day. For Guardi, on the other hand, the buildings, although not carelessly drawn, were essentially a background that reflects or obstructs the slanting light, to provide that early evening effect of pinks and blues, glowing lights and dusky

shadows, which Guardi loved to paint. In the square are gathered small clusters of figures muffled in their tricorn hats and cloaks, and possibly wearing their masks, as if busily planning their evening's diversion.

Although eighteenth-century Venice was a pale shadow of the great maritime power that had once been the "bridge of the sea" and a notable center for Renaissance painters, the Venetians still clung to their ancient traditions, and every year the state barge continued to make its pilgrimage to San Niccolò di Lido. This ceremony was called "the wedding of Venice to the sea," and the Doge cast a golden ring into the Adriatic to pay homage to the sea, which had long been the source of Venetian wealth and power. This pilgrimage could have had little meaning in Guardi's day, for the great trading fleets had vanished years before; yet Guardi painted the state barge (Plate 1-78) with all the jauntiness and charm it must have possessed two hundred years earlier. Unfortunately, Francesco Guardi was himself the last of the great Venetian painters.

1-78. *The Departure of the State Barge* (detail), by Francesco Guardi

Spain

UNDER CHARLES V, the forces of Hapsburg Spain had held Italy subject in the sixteenth century, but by the seventeenth century Spain herself was in decline, suffering from the same shortsighted and corrupt government with which she controlled her empire in Italy. The three Hapsburg rulers of the century—Philip III, Philip IV, and Charles II—were weak and were influenced by whatever courtier's ideas were favored at the moment. These seventeenth-century monarchs were blinded by the glamour of Spain's past, in the great age of explorations and conquest, and they failed to see that her greatness could only be retained by a revival of agriculture and industry at home. Instead, they undertook a number of imprudent moves and, having started with their empire intact, in the course of the century they lost first Portugal and then Catalonia, regained the Netherlands only with difficulty, and eventually lost their Italian possessions, Minorca, and Gibraltar.

But the general decadence of Spain in the seventeenth century was overlaid with an ironic flowering of artistic genius. Although a dismal period of failure both at home and abroad, this decline, strangely enough, was portrayed in some of the greatest paintings and writings in Spain's history. This was, in fact, the "golden age" of Spanish literature, the era of Cervantes' *Don Quixote,* the greatest of what are called "picaresque" novels. The *pícaro* was usually a kind of rogue or vagabond, meant to be a social outcast who saw life from the outside and who, as he passed from situation to situation, pricked the bubbles of Spanish pride and delusion.

Spain was the most deeply religious country in Europe and was powerfully bound to the Church of Rome; yet the baroque art of Spain differed in its own peculiar way from that of Counter Reformation Italy. As was so often the case with Spanish art, architecture in Spain wavered between the two extremes of a desire for excess and the tendency toward harsh austerity. Structures such as the Clock Tower of the Cathedral of Santiago de Compostela (Plate 2-1), designed by Domingo de Andrade (c. 1639–1712), have harder outlines than the free-flowing curves and spirals of the Italian baroque; yet the surface decoration is even more elaborate

2-1. Clock Tower, Cathedral of Santiago de Compostela, by Domingo de Andrade

than anything to be seen in Italy. Moreover, the delicate tracery of interweaving patterns shows the influence of the Moors, who, although exiled from Spain a hundred years before, had left behind architectural monuments of great beauty.

Sculpture was created largely to adorn churches, and seventeenth-century sculptors usually concentrated on life-sized figures in the round, intended for the decoration of chapels and altars. Spain had long been strangely conservative in art, and such statuary was usually made of wood and elaborately painted—a fashion that had gone out of style in much of Western Europe a hundred years before.

Spanish sculptors absorbed many of the lessons of the Italian baroque style, in particular, the sense that a closer relationship could exist between the spectator and the work of art. But the very desire to create work endowed with the greatest expressive power and to involve the viewer in the reality of the scene led to excesses, both emotional and technical, of a kind which Bernini would never have allowed. Colored glass embedded in painted wooden drapery, to simulate material embroidered with jewels, glass eyes, genuine clothing, eyelashes made of hair, wigs—all of these are found in Spanish sculpture of this period.

Exemplifying these peculiarly Spanish excesses is the work of Gregorio Hernández (1576–1636), who spent much of his life at Valladolid, in northern Spain. Concentrating on religious imagery throughout his career, he specialized in episodes from the life of Christ. He made single figures and *pasos,* which are groups of five or six figures that are arranged in a theatrical tableau and carried in street processions during Holy Week ceremonies. Hernández paid great attention to realistic effects in his *Pietà* (Plate 2-2),[1] taking care to differentiate between the pallor of the dead Christ's flesh and the skin of the living Madonna. Although remarkably lifelike in such surface details,

---

[1] A conventional artistic form in which the Virgin is portrayed mourning over the body of the dead Christ.

2-2. *Pietà* (detail), by Gregorio Hernández

2-3. *Martyrdom of St. Bartholomew* (detail), by José Ribera

2-4. *Drunken Silenus* (detail), by José Ribera

Hernández' works have all the exaggerated, affectedly posed emotion found in much Italian baroque sculpture.

Yet, for all the fantasy and theatricality of Spanish architecture and sculpture, and the Spanish fascination with religion and spiritual matters, Spain produced during the seventeenth century three painters outstanding for their direct and ruthless realism: José (Jusepe de) Ribera (1591–1652), Francisco de Zurbarán (1598–1664), and the master of the age, Diego Velázquez (1599–1660). All three were influenced, in one way or another, by the dark, "realistic" paintings of Caravaggio.

Born at Játiva, near Valencia, Ribera was the son of a shoemaker. At an unknown date he went to Lombardy, and from there to Rome. By 1616 he had settled in Naples, where he served successive Spanish viceroys until his death. The fact that he spent most of his working life in Naples did not affect Ribera's position as the most important Spanish painter in the early part of the seventeenth century, because his paintings

2-5. *Jacob's Dream,* by José Ribera

were sent back to Spain in sufficient quantities for his talent to be appreciated and his influence felt. He was able to turn from mythology to religious subjects without difficulty, and sweet devotional images came to his brush as readily as the anguished scenes of martyrdom (Plate 2-3) that appealed to Spanish taste; these he produced in large quantities with the aid of pupils.

In his day Ribera was considered a follower of Caravaggio, whose works he had studied in Rome. His early paintings, such as the *Drunken Silenus* (Plate 2-4), have all of Caravaggio's deeply shadowed reality. Silenus (in classical mythology an aged woodland deity, part man and part beast, and a follower of Dionysus, god of wine) is seen as a sweating and panting inebriate, with traces of beard and an addled expression. As in the greatest of Caravaggio's paintings, Ribera has portrayed an imaginary subject in strongly realistic terms. Later in his career, as can be seen in his *Jacob's Dream* (Plate 2-5), while he remained true to Caravaggio's realism in portraying Jacob as an altogether recognizable individual, Ribera painted more delicately, with cooler tonalities and lighter colors and backgrounds.

At the beginning of the seventeenth century painting flourished in Seville, and it was here that the talents of both Zurbarán and Velázquez developed. But the two artists were not alike. Zurbarán represents Spanish art at its most severe. Unlike Velázquez, he was never a "court artist," despite some commissions from the court, but concentrated on religious pictures in a most serious vein. In paintings such as his *Three Saints* or his *St. Apollonia* (invoked against toothache and usually represented holding a tooth in pincers as a sign of her martyrdom; Plates 2-6, 2-7), we can see how his solid figures, with their sharply modeled drapery, were influenced by the painted

2-6. *Three Saints,* by Francisco de Zurbarán

wood sculpture of the period. This is true, too, of his magnificent painting *The Corpse of St. Bonaventura Displayed* (Plate 2-8), although here one is more aware of his fascination with the surface texture of cloth. Again the scene is illuminated by the dark and dramatic lighting of Caravaggio, but its quiet sanctity is suggested chiefly by the sensitive gestures of the mourners' hands. It is curious that, in the manner of Caravaggio's early still life, Zurbarán also liked to detail painstakingly a few selected objects against a dark background (Plate 2-9).

With the help of assistants, Zurbarán maintained a large output of paintings, many of which were sent to the Spanish colonies in the New World. Nevertheless, though famous in his lifetime and flatteringly referred to by the Spanish king Philip IV as "painter to the King, and the king of painters," Zurbarán was all but forgotten in the century after his death and was not recalled until the looting of the Napoleonic wars brought many of his works out of their monastic seclusion.

Although Velázquez was to become one of the greatest of European portrait painters, he did not begin his career as a portraitist. Born in Seville in 1599, he was apprenticed at the age of twelve to Francisco Pacheco (1564–1654), a mediocre local painter of predominantly religious subjects. This apprenticeship ended in 1617, and a year later Velázquez married Pacheco's daughter.

Almost all of Velázquez' early works are either religious in theme, such as his painting of St. Thomas (Plate 2-10), or illustrations of everyday popular life. Genre scenes of this type, known in Spanish as *bodegones* (from the word meaning "eating place" or "tavern"), usually featured people eating and often included impressive still-life displays of food. These were very popular in Seville at the beginning of the seventeenth century. Velázquez' style in dealing with these subjects—dwelling on the ordinary, excluding all that is idealized, and with an emphasis on highlights and strong shadow—is like Caravaggio's, although one important difference between Caravaggio and Velázquez should be noted. If *The Water Seller of Seville* (Plate 2-11) or the *Old Woman Cooking Eggs* (Plate 2-12) were to be compared with, for example, Caravaggio's *Gypsy Fortuneteller* (Plate 1-7), it would be seen that Velázquez

was far more interested in defining, with the greatest precision, the peculiar texture and exact appearance of each surface, whether skin or glass, metal or leather. At this he was an even greater master than Zurbarán, and one can readily overlook his other technical imperfections—the perspective of the lower part of both these compositions is too steep, for instance. It has also been pointed out that, whereas Velázquez' treatment of textures is perfect, it sometimes seems as if his figures, such as the boy handing a glass to the water carrier, lack a bone structure beneath their flesh, almost as if their surfaces might simply be blown up with air from within. The greatness of these works, which might otherwise have been thought trivial because of their subject matter, was appreciated by Pacheco, who felt honored to have been Velázquez' teacher:

> Are we then to hold these *bodegones* as of no account? No, they are certainly to be valued— that is, when painted as Velázquez paints them—for in this branch he has attained such eminence that he has left room for no rival. They deserve high esteem, for with these elements and with portraiture he discovered the true imitation of Nature, and encouraged many by his powerful example.... The figures must be ably drawn and painted, and must appear as lifelike and inanimate Nature; then they will reflect the highest honor on their authors.[2]

In any case, Velázquez realized that he would do better to establish his name as an outstanding genre painter than to attempt more ambitious subjects. When asked why he did not paint more serious matter, in the style of Raphael and the Renaissance masters, he replied: "I would rather be the first in this coarse stuff than second in nicety."

2 Francisco Pacheco, *El arte de la pintura, su antigüedad y grandeza* ("The Art of Painting, Its Antiquity and Greatness"), Seville, 1649.

Velázquez' preoccupation with specific textures and a vivid realism link him with the tradition of Zurbarán and Ribera, and even with the wood sculptors of seventeenth-century Spain. What, then, sets Velázquez apart and justifies the claim that he is the greatest of Spanish painters? For one thing, sheer skill and exceptional powers of observation helped his style. He had a sharper eye for the appearance of things, and his figures and compositions are so supple that those of Zurbarán seem wooden by comparison. But even more important than Velázquez' skill and perception was the way in which these came to influence his general approach to painting. Hernández' *Pietà* (Plate 2-2) was designed to create a realistic effect; but its actual character is very artificial, for while the details are naturalistic, the poses and gestures seem exaggerated and unnatural. It is no small part of Velázquez' greatness as an artist that he was always trying to eliminate precisely this kind of contradiction. It seemed important to him that the picture as a whole, the grouping of the figures, their stance, and their relationship in space—the total vision, in short—should be treated in the same fashion as the details of accessory objects and costume. This aim, of course, created certain problems. If it allowed Velázquez to become an incomparable painter of portraits from life, it made him a less satisfactory interpreter of themes from the imagination. He painted very few religious pictures later in his career, and almost all of these, although brilliantly painted, have a posed, studio air.

Velázquez was precocious, and his talent was quickly recognized. In the spring of 1623, he was summoned to Madrid by the Count-Duke Olivares, Philip IV's powerful minister. He painted portraits (now lost) of the King and of the visiting Prince of Wales (later Charles I), which were much

2-7. *St. Apollonia,* by Francisco de Zurbarán

67

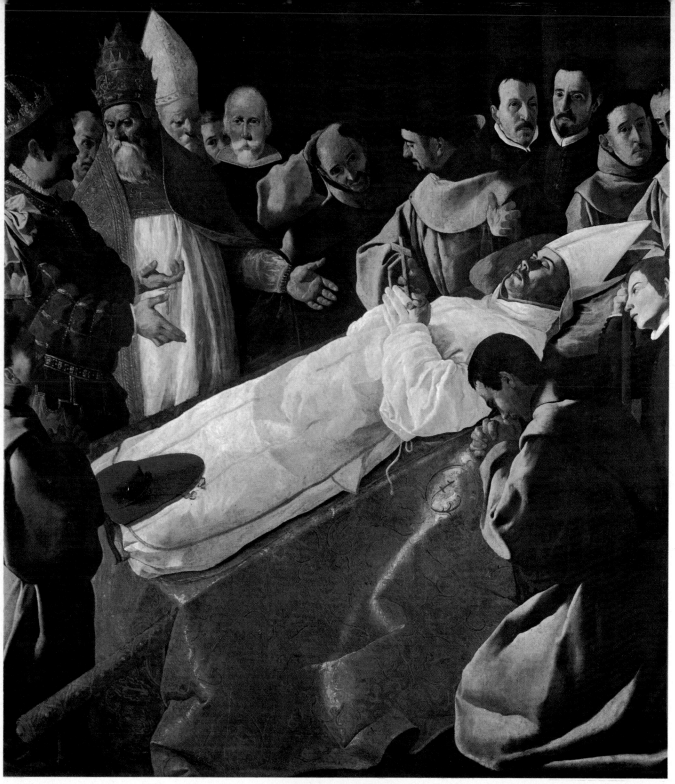

2-8.   *The Corpse of St. Bonaventura Displayed,* by Francisco de Zurbarán

2-9.   *Still Life,*
by Francisco de Zurbarán

admired. The artist was ordered to transfer his household to Madrid, and on October 2, 1623, Velázquez was formally appointed Royal Painter. This was the beginning of a lifetime of service to Philip IV, who treated the painter with a touching disregard for the rigid social conventions of the day. Velázquez was given increasingly important posts at court, and he died in the King's service in the summer of 1660. Thus Velázquez spent the greater part of his life setting down, in the minutest detail, the court life of the tragic reign of Philip IV.

Philip IV came to the throne at the age of sixteen and for twenty years was completely under the influence of his chamberlain, the Count-Duke Olivares, with disastrous results. The monarch was a desperately religious man and gloomy in temperament; indeed, it was said that he laughed only three times in his life. His first wife and most of his children died, and he was left with an heir who was weak-minded and so feeble that he could not walk until he was seven. This unfortunate child, moreover, had so pronounced a "Hapsburg" jutting jaw that he could not chew his food. The tone of the court was violently religious and morbidly melancholy, with a complement of jesters and dwarfs providing diversion for its warped tastes.

Velázquez' position at court was in itself extraordinary. In the words of the historian Jean Descola,

Diego Rodriguez de Silva y Velasquez pursued two careers simultaneously: he was Philip IV's quartermaster general and official court painter. . . . He painted not only the King, but the Infante [Prince] Don Carlos, the Infante-Cardinal Fernando, the King's sister Maria, his first wife, Elizabeth of Bourbon, and his son Baltasar Carlos. All the models died, and the King remarried. Velasquez painted Philip's

2-10. *St. Thomas* (detail), by Diego Velázquez

2-11. *The Water Seller of Seville,*
by Diego Velázquez

second wife, Mariana of Austria, and her daughter, the Infanta [Princess] Marguerita. But the demands of his art did not distract him from his duties as quartermaster general. It was he who arranged the meeting between the royal families of France and Spain after the Treaty of the Pyrenees [1660] and prepared the way for the marriage of Louis XIV and the Infanta Maria Theresa of Austria. Cold, formal, reserved, he was a courtier who attended every festivity and whose elegant attire won the praise of Princes. His clothes were adorned with Milanese lace.... He wore the red cross of his order and an engraved silver badge, and carried a very handsome short sword of state . . . a small diamond-encrusted coat of arms with the habit [order] of Santiago in inlaid enamel hung from a chain around his neck. Such was Velasquez when he lived at close quarters with the royal couple on the Island of Pheasants in the Bidassoa. He also had more prosaic duties—paying for the firewood and the service of chimney sweeps, supervising the maintenance of lamps, the setting of tables and the preparation of guest rooms, seeing to the last details, even to the placing of chamber pots in the bedrooms. Both steward and major-domo, Velasquez could hardly

fail to profit by this unique opportunity to live with his models . . . withdrawing to his studio, he merely reproduced on canvas the traits and gestures of his hosts."[3]

Velázquez' main task as court painter was to paint portraits of the royal family and their relations and of prominent courtiers. But he was also called upon to paint the court dwarfs and jesters, mythological pictures to decorate the royal palaces, religious scenes for the royal chapels, or, as in *The Surrender of Breda* (Plate 2-13), canvases glorifying the achievements of Spain. He also looked after the royal art collections.

In Velázquez' early works, the realism is detailed and unsparing. This was hardly a style suitable for flattering royal portraiture, and Velázquez did in fact modify his manner somewhat, making it less relentlessly realistic.

Although he was a court painter, he did not wish to suggest that people, whether aristocrats or commoners, were essentially noble or heroic. No great artist has ever had so few axes to grind. Velázquez simply tried to record what he saw in front of him objectively and accurately, without being deliberately unkind. He saw that shadows have color in them. He set that down. He saw that Philip IV had a weak face with a heavy jaw and watery eyes that got sadder as the king aged, and he recorded the change as the years passed. Above all, he maintained his naturally posed compositions. *The Surrender of Breda,* for example, was painted to celebrate the victory of the Spanish general Ambrogio Spinola, who laid seige to this principal stronghold of the Spanish Netherlands, which had been captured by the Dutch in their struggle to free themselves from the government of Spain.

2-12. *Old Woman Cooking Eggs* (detail), by Diego Velázquez

[3] Jean Descola, *A History of Spain* (trans. from the French by E. P. Halperin), Alfred A. Knopf, New York, 1963.

Still, though a composition of monumental scale, there are no exaggeratedly theatrical poses. Spinola is seen accepting the keys from the vanquished Justin of Nassau with a simple gesture, as one gentleman to another. The grandeur of Spain is powerfully suggested in the most understated way: the defeated Dutch on the left seem a pathetic and motley crew when compared with the proud army of Spain on the right, represented by a forest of upright lances.

The same unposed and natural effect is the secret of Velázquez' *Las Meninas* ("The Maids of Honor"; Plate 2-14), one of the most famous of his portraits of the royal family. The picture shows the Infanta Doña Margarita with her ladies-in-waiting, the court jester Nicolasito, the female dwarf María Bárbola, and a pet mastiff in a room of the Alcázar Palace in Madrid. Exactly what is happening in this picture remains to this day uncertain, but several explanations have been offered. Was Velázquez in the act of painting a portrait of the Infanta's parents when the child and her retinue entered the room and so entranced him that he turned to painting them instead? It may be that the princess was unwilling to join her parents posing for the painter, and one of her maids of honor, Doña María Augustina Sarmiento, who offers her a small red flask, perhaps containing chocolate or perfumed water, may be attempting to persuade her. The entire scene is in a way a brilliant visual trick. The King and Queen, probably posing for the painter, are in the position of the actual viewer and are represented in the picture merely by their reflection in a mirror behind the Infanta. The group not only is casually posed (the chamberlain, Don José Nieto, seems to be just leaving the room) but appears as if caught in a very transitory action. Above all, by his highly sensitive use of color in portraying the muted shades of surfaces at varying distances, Velázquez creates the atmosphere of the musty air in a room of the palace, illuminated by three sources of light (two windows not seen on the right and the hallway at the back), and an almost uncanny effect of physical depth. It was popularly said that Velázquez had "painted air." Theophile Gautier, the nineteenth-century French man of letters, asked simply, "But where is the picture?"

Still, Velázquez was capable—when he chose—of creating the most dramatic and unreal of compositions, as in his equestrian portrait of Prince Baltasar Carlos (Plate 2-15), the unfortunate heir of Philip IV. Not only is the little prince flatteringly, even dashingly portrayed, but here the style of painting itself is very different from his usual manner of painting. The forms are altogether softer than they are in *The Water Seller of Seville* (Plate 2-11), for example; and if one stands very close to the canvas, the details look blurred. During the 1630's Velázquez concentrated on presenting scenes as they actually appeared at a moment's

71

2-14. *Las Meninas,* by Diego Velázquez

2-15. *Prince Baltasar Carlos on Horseback,* by Diego Velázquez

grasp. His earlier works were realistic and very impressive; yet their content was treated with a kind of artificial impartiality, for the eye does not naturally see every element of a scene, all at once, with such clarity. Velázquez began to suggest figures and objects with a few bold strokes of the brush, as they might be seen at a casual glance. His painting *Garden of the Villa Medici in Rome* (Plate 2-16) is in this freer style. (Velázquez visited Italy twice, in the years 1629–1631 and again in 1649–1651, when this landscape was probably produced.) It is hard to believe that his picture entitled *Las Hilanderas* ("The Spinners"; Plate 2-17), which illustrates the myth of Arachne, the woman of Lydia whom Athena turned into a spider, was created by the same artist who painted *The Water Seller.* In the former, a much later work, the painter has adopted bold, free strokes. The spinners' hands are suggested with only a few daubs of paint, which give them a feeling of motion. The figures in the background are even more

2-16. *Garden of the Villa Medici in Rome,*
by Diego Velázquez

sketchily painted. This loose brushwork resembles the style of the impressionists more than two centuries later. It is because of his natural compositions and his study of such visual effects in painting that Velázquez was not only the most outstanding Spanish artist of his day but also a great innovator—truly one of the fathers of modern painting.

Although no other painter emerged in the second half of the seventeenth century to challenge Velázquez' supreme stature as an artist, the demand for pictures of every type, from large-scale altarpieces to intimate still life, was met by a great number of talented practitioners. The best-known among these was Bartolomé Esteban Murillo (1617–1682), a barber-surgeon's son who created the Seville Academy of Painting in 1660. Murillo's delicately colored and highly sentimental religious paintings (Plate 2-18) were in such demand in Spain and Spanish America that he was eventually more successful than Zurbarán, who was still working in Seville. His genre pictures, for example, his very popular painting *Boys Eating Melons and Grapes* (Plate 2-19), seem overly sweet and sentimental when compared with Velázquez' treatment of similar subjects but, nonetheless, were much admired in the centuries after Murillo's death.

During the eighteenth century, Spain's decline as a world power continued. The Hapsburg line of the monarchy in Spain came to an end in 1700, with the death of the feeble and ailing Charles II, under whom the country had sunk to the lowest level of prestige in its history. He left no heirs, and the French king, Louis XIV, ambitious for territory in Spain, passed on the claims that he had through his wife, Charles I's half sister, to his grandson Philip. The new king, Philip V, a boy of seventeen, was des-

2-17. *Las Hilanderas* (detail),
by Diego Velázquez

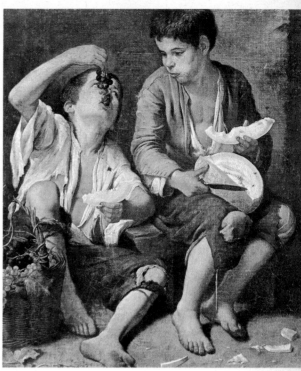

2-19. *Boys Eating Melons and Grapes* (detail), by Bartolomé Esteban Murillo

2-18. *Christ as the Good Shepherd,* by Bartolomé Esteban Murillo

tined to reign for forty-six years. In 1702 he married Maria Louisa of Savoy, who died in 1714, leaving behind four sons. In December of that year, Philip V took as his wife Elizabeth Farnese of Parma, an insatiably ambitious woman who completely dominated her husband and who was to be a powerful force in Spain for half a century. The French-born king, reared at Versailles, and his Italian wife tended to impose their native tastes upon their new kingdom, especially in the arts. The position of favorite court painter was held by one French artist after another; Philip V's successor, Charles III, brought first the Italianate German painter, Anton Raffael Mengs (1728–1779), to Madrid, and then Giovanni Battista Tiepolo. Meanwhile, talented Spanish artists such as the still-life painter Louis Egidio Meléndez (1716–1780; Plate 2-20) were

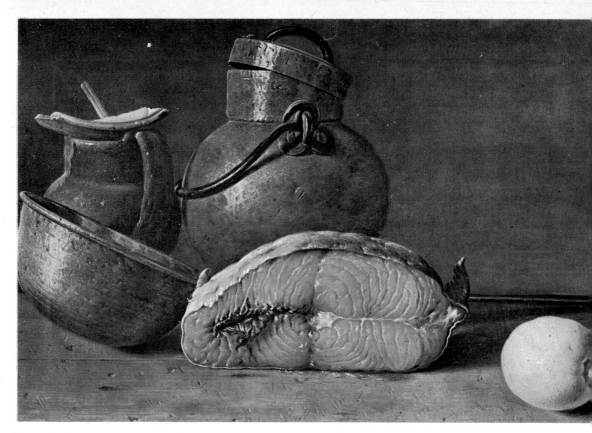

2-20. *Still Life with Salmon and Lemon,* by Luis Egidio Meléndez

neglected. Meléndez, in his own words, claimed he "had not the means even to nourish himself, his brush being his only asset."

The architecture and architectural decoration of the period went beyond all previous bounds. Architects such as Pedro de Ribera (c. 1683–1742; Plate 2-21); Narciso Tomé (active by 1715–d. 1742; Plate 2-22), with his father and brothers; and the influential Churriguera family (Plate 2-23), especially José Benito (1665–1725), carried the baroque tradition of Borromini to new heights of elaborate and fantastic invention in many of their works. When one looks at the creations of these men, beautiful and incredibly rich as they are, it is easy to see why to more sober foreign critics they appeared to be "delirious fools."

In painting, it was not until the end of the eighteenth century that Spain produced another painter to rival Velázquez' genius. This was Francisco de Goya y Lucientes (1746–1828); the son of a master gilder, he rose to be first painter of the court and became possibly the most striking artistic genius in all Europe at the turn of the nineteenth century. Goya, too, was unlike Velázquez in that he was an impassioned man, deeply interested in social problems—an artist who was not able, thus, to record the visual appearance of his subjects with cool detachment and without personal

2-21. Doorway of the Hospicio de San Fernando, Madrid, by Pedro de Ribera

comment. His royal portraits are harsh, almost caricature portrayals of the members of a society he despised. Later in his career, depressed by a serious illness and the resulting deafness, he turned to painting tortured, nightmare fantasies full of the horrors he saw and felt around him. If Velázquez suggested the decay of the Spanish court of his day by a straightforward portrayal of external appearances, Goya left no doubts in his presentation; yet, like Velázquez, he was a superb technician. Moreover, Goya also was an innovator, whose ability to convey his own anguished inner vision gave him greater affinity with the emerging nineteenth-century art and the romantic movement than with the refined and delicate rococo style, which had dominated much of eighteenth-century art and which, early in his career, he had briefly acknowledged in his highly decorative, exquisitely colored tapestry cartoons (designs).[4]

[4] The life and works of Francisco de Goya y Lucientes are given full treatment and illustrations of his work can be found in the author's *Nineteenth Century Art,* part of the "Discovering Art" series.

2-23. Main Altar of the Seminary, Salamanca, by the Churriguera family

2-22. The *Transparente* Altar, Cathedral of Toledo, by Narciso Tomé

The Netherlands and Germany

THE NORTHERN STATES, the United Provinces of the Netherlands, popularly known as Holland, broke away from Spanish rule at the beginning of the seventeenth century; but the southern region, thereafter known as the Spanish Netherlands (present-day Belgium), continued for a long time to be part of the Spanish empire. In the shadow of the newly independent states to the north, which were Protestant, the Spanish Netherlands became more deeply Catholic, with the result that its artists enjoyed many opportunities denied to their contemporaries in Holland, where the Protestant churches were for the most part left undecorated. In the Spanish Netherlands—the area often referred to as Flanders because of its most prosperous province—as in Italy, painting and sculpture were considered important instruments for the illustration of church doctrine. Thus Peter Paul Rubens (1577–1640), the greatest Flemish artist of the age, found generous outlet for his talents in the many large altarpieces and the symbolic religious works ordered by Catholic patrons.

In spite of the links between the Spanish empire and Italy, a truly baroque style of architecture never developed in Flanders. Since the rulers of the Spanish Netherlands continued to live in Brussels in medieval palaces, domestic architecture did not receive the inspiration and patronage of a wealthy court, as it did in France and Spain. In Flanders the principles of baroque design were confined to decorative, ornamental detail. The seventeenth-century houses of the Grand' Place in Brussels (Plate 3-1) are typical. In these, pilasters (flattened pillars attached, or "engaged," to a wall surface) and classical figures, scrolls, garlands, and vase motifs—all the favorite decorative patterns of baroque architecture—have been applied to tall, steep-roofed houses completely medieval in character, which were constructed in a style that had been in use for some four hundred years.

In painting the situation was very different. Throughout the sixteenth century, Flemish artists had come increasingly under the spell of Italian art. This movement toward the adoption of the Italian sense of idealized form reached its height in the career of Rubens, the greatest exemplar of the full baroque style in Northern Europe, and the only true Northern counterpart to Bernini.

3-1. Houses in the Grand' Place, Brussels

In his childhood, Rubens served as page in the household of Margaret of Ligne-Aremberg, in East Flanders. This was followed by several years' study with three masters, all of whom were strongly under the influence of Italian art. In 1598 Rubens became a master of the Antwerp guild, and in the following year he was working as an assistant on the scenery for the ceremonial entry into Antwerp of Archduke Albert and the Infanta Isabella, the Spanish rulers of the Netherlands. Thus, at an early age he was already familiar with the conduct of court life, as well as with the organization and maintenance of a large studio with many assistants.

From 1600 to 1608 Rubens lived in Italy, where he was court painter to the Gonzagas in Mantua. News of his mother's illness brought him back to Antwerp, but he arrived too late to see her alive. Although he never returned to Italy, Rubens was by now a brilliant painter in the Italian style. During the next year (1609) there occurred two events that shaped his life: he was appointed court painter to Archduke Albert and his consort Isabella, and he married the charming Isabella Brandt. When the Archduke died in 1621, Rubens was taken increasingly into the confidence of the widowed Infanta, who began to employ him on diplomatic missions. He was, in fact, a perfect courtier—handsome, with a blond mustache and fine features, famous for his charm, and a superb linguist. His extensive correspondence shows him to have been a scholar, antiquarian, dabbler in science, humanist, and family man. That he was also a very great painter made him one of the wonders of the age.

In 1626 Rubens's wife died. Four years later he married the sixteen-year-old Hélène Fourment, the daughter of a silk merchant and the niece of his late wife. Rather than a lady of the court, he chose, as he himself put it, "one who would not blush to see me take my brushes in hand." Meanwhile, his diplomatic activities had increased in the late 1620's, with lengthy visits to Spain (1628), where he met Velázquez, and to England (1629), where he was knighted by Charles I and also received a degree from Cambridge University. Moreover, at the same time, his studio was turning out a wealth of commissions for the church and the foremost Catholic monarchs of Europe, as well as for private clients. Rubens himself would often merely sketch the design for a painting to be executed by his assistants, and would then add the finishing touches. This enabled him to produce a vast number of works, and so telling and perfect were his "finishing touches" that almost all the canvases which he signed were of unquestionable excellence.

Rubens's talent knew no limitations. He admired the works of many painters of many schools and filled his Italianate palace in Antwerp, and later his country home, with paintings by the Italian masters, Titian, Tintoretto, and Veronese, as well as those by painters of the Northern Renaissance such as Jan van Eyck and Pieter Bruegel. In his own style Rubens tried to combine the best of both strains—the grandiose compositions full of monumental figures and stately movement created to satisfy the Italian Renaissance and baroque tastes, and the meticulous rendering of surface texture and the small accidents of lifelike detail that the painters of the Northern Renaissance developed so impressively. His canvases were often huge, and his ability to create fantastically complicated, superb compositions on any theme was astounding. He could turn from the painting of mythological and religious subject matter to portraits, landscapes, and genre and hunting scenes. Above all, Rubens's pictures breathed a marvelous vitality in the brilliant, translucent color for which he was famous— splendid shades of red and warm, glossy flesh tones. His figures always seem to glow with health, to be full of robust, sparkling life.

A self-portrait of this extraordinary man is to be seen on the left of his painting entitled simply *Four Philosophers* (Plate 3-2). The other sitters are (from left to right): the artist's brother Philip; Justus Lipsius, the Flemish authority on Roman literature, history, and antiquities, who had in fact died several years before this portrait of the imaginary quartet was painted; and Jan Wouverius, a Flemish humanist scholar and a pupil of Lipsius.

Rubens was the most successful artist of the age, and as can be imagined, his huge canvases were ideally suited for decorating the many palaces that were constructed or enlarged during the seventeenth century. Moreover, his attachment to the church and to the idea of monarchy made him an ideal choice as painter to royalty. Rubens worked for Philip IV of Spain and Charles I of England, and in 1622 Marie de Médicis of France commissioned him to paint twenty-one large canvases illustrating, in allegorical form, the chief events of her life. Allegory in art is the portrayal of events in terms of symbolic figures that represent thoughts and concepts, and Rubens was particularly brilliant at devising allegorical means of presenting any idea or situation. These pictures were intended to decorate a gallery of the Luxembourg Palace in Paris. With extensive use of studio assistants, the commission was completed by 1625, and in February of that year Rubens went to Paris to supervise the installation of the paintings. The scene from the cycle illustrated here shows the future queen (the bride of Henri IV) disembarking at Marseilles (Plate 3-3). She is received by allegorical figures representing France and the city of Marseilles. In the sea are symbolic marine dieties who have ensured the betrothed's safety throughout her voyage. It is typical of Rubens, with his love of both the classically idealized and precise detail, that he should have combined in one glorious scene heroic nudes and figures in elaborate contemporary costume.

His works for the church were no less important. His study entitled *The Triumph of the Church* (Plate 3-4) is a preparatory oil sketch for the design of a tapestry, one of a set intended for the Convent of the Royal Barefoot Sisterhood in Madrid. Here the Catholic Church, allegorically represented carrying the Holy Sacrament, is borne in a chariot riding over the fallen powers of Fury, Discord, and Hatred, while the figures of Blindness (with eyes bandaged) and Ignorance are yoked behind. In the foreground, the globe is seen encircled by a snake biting its own tail, which represents Evil. The horses of the chariot are led triumphantly by the figures of the Cardinal Virtues. What is most amazing is that the entire complicated allegory is worked into a glowing, marvelously intricate yet harmonious design.

Rubens was equally successful with simple and intimate portraits of members of his family. He was particularly fond of painting his second wife and their children, whom he used either as straight portrait sitters or as models for narrative scenes. His painting of *Hélène Fourment and Her Children* (Plate 3-5) is probably meant as an informal, private portrait, but in composition it is close to being a painting of the Madonna.

Rubens was always interested in landscape, but this was particularly true in the 1630's, when he bought a country estate known as the Château of Steen, where he settled for the last five years of his life. Paintings such as his *Landscape on the River Polder* and *Peasants Returning from the Fields* (Plates 3-6, 3-7) show a very real love of nature as he saw it in Flanders, although somewhat idealized. Still, it is baroque decoration, and the figures of the peasants in the latter painting have more the look of graceful dancers in a ballet than of actual tillers of the soil.

Rubens dominated Flemish painting during the seventeenth century, and the two greatest painters that Flanders produced in the next generation had both served as his pupils and assistants. These were Anthony (Anton) van Dyck (1599–1641), who barely outlived his master, and Jacob Jordaens (1593–1678).

Van Dyck, like Rubens knighted by Charles I, was born in Antwerp and became Rubens's chief assistant while still in his teens. He absorbed the elaborate Rubensian style, which he practiced in the studio, and also on his own account, but which he was never able to carry off with quite the same success as his master. Introspective and withdrawn, Van Dyck lacked Rubens's robust spirit. His major historical and religious pictures are always virtuoso in handling, but they give the impression that the artist's effort to be heroic was costing too much. Only in more simple compositions involving fewer figures, such as the Holy Family in the *Rest on the Flight into Egypt* (Plate 3-8), in which he could stress grace and softness, was he wholly successful as a narrative painter.

His natural talent was for portraiture, and he first appeared as a distinguished artist in his own right during a stay in Italy in his early twenties, when he painted a series of elegant and dignified portraits, among them a self-portrait (Plate 3-9). Van Dyck spent the years 1627–1632 back in Antwerp, where

3-2. *Four Philosophers* (detail), by Peter Paul Rubens

in portraits such as that of Jan de Wael and his wife (Plate 3-10) he perfected his style and adapted it to the simpler tastes and directness of his Flemish merchant sitters.

In 1632 Van Dyck left Flanders for England, where he lived for the rest of his short life and where he became court painter to Charles I. This appointment was one of the most fitting and fruitful in the history

3-4. *The Triumph of the Church,* by Peter Paul Rubens

of European art, and in his official capacity Van Dyck succeeded in immortalizing the great figures of the entire period. Possessing a sensitive, elegant, yet free technique, he had exactly the qualities King Charles was searching for in a painter. With such royal favor, it is hardly surprising that Van Dyck should have become the preferred painter of the English aristocracy. The result was such a heavy demand for his portraits, often including replicas intended for various members of a family, that he was only able to fulfill all his commissions by running a large studio and employing assistants.

Although many of Van Dyck's English portraits are weak, largely studio productions, there is a hard core of signed work by the artist himself that can stand comparison with any paintings produced in Europe in the seventeenth century. The oval portrait of Sir Endymion Porter shows the sitter, a prominent courtier and friend of both Rubens and Van Dyck, posed with the artist himself (Plate 3-11). Van Dyck heightened the poetic mood in this, as in many of his late portraits, by the inclusion of an evening landscape. The work is a very fine example and displays the elegance, beauty of color, and delicacy of handling of Van Dyck at his best. This is true as well of his warmly golden portrait of William II, Prince of Orange, Charles I's sixteen-year-old son-in-law (Plate 3-12).

Jacob Jordaens lived most of his life in

3-3. *The Reception of Marie de Médicis at Marseilles,* by Peter Paul Rubens

3-5. *Hélène Fourment and Her Children,* by Peter Paul Rubens

3-6. *Landscape on the River Polder,*
by Peter Paul Rubens

3-7. *Peasants Returning from the Fields* (detail), by Peter Paul Rubens

3-8. *Rest on the Flight into Egypt,*
by Anthony van Dyck

3-10. *Jan de Wael and His Wife,*
by Anthony van Dyck

3-9. *Self-portrait,*
by Anthony van Dyck

Antwerp, and from first to last his works reveal the influence of Rubens, in composition, figure types, and coloring. In the 1630's, when Rubens himself participated less and less in the large commissions he accepted, Jordaens proved extremely useful in carrying out pictures that either were signed by Rubens or were independently signed but painted from a Rubens design.

Jordaens profited greatly from the deaths, almost within the span of a year, of Rubens and Van Dyck. When Rubens died in 1640, the painter Balthasar Gerbier could write of Jordaens as "prime painter here." Van Dyck's death in the following year eliminated the one artist whom Jordaens might regard as a rival. Jordaens was then left in the enviable position of being able to pick and choose among the commissions that flooded in.

Jordaens inherited Rubens's opportunities and produced, with a similar participation of assistants, a large and varied output of paintings; but he never achieved Rubens's Olympian quality. His painting *Meleager and Atalanta* (Plate 3-13) represents Meleager, who was the son of the Queen of Calydonia, presenting the pelt of the Calydonian boar, which he has slain, to his beloved Atalanta, while his uncles, who claim the pelt for their own, rage in the background. As is readily seen, the differences between master and pupil are enormous. Where Rubens's colors glow, those of Jordaens merely shine, and where Rubens's figures are vibrant and full of life, those of Jordaens seem heavy and posed.

Another assistant of Rubens should be mentioned. Frans Snyders (1597–1657), who painted the still-life sections of many of

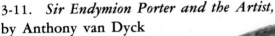

3-11. *Sir Endymion Porter and the Artist,* by Anthony van Dyck

Rubens's works, succeeded in bringing the principles of monumental, Rubens-like composition to still-life painting (Plate 3-14). But still life, as a form of painting, was far more important to the artistic life of Holland than to the Flemish world of Rubens.

During the first half of the seventeenth century the Dutch economy witnessed an enormous expansion. Trade increased, scientific methods of agriculture were developed, potterymaking and bulb growing were taken up on a large scale, and Amsterdam became a center for banking and the diamond trade. It was at this time that Holland became the center of a colonial empire. By 1650, the Dutch navy was beginning to constitute a serious threat to England's maritime supremacy. The rise of a large and prosperous merchant class created a demand for "modest" luxury goods, small in scale and unpretentious.

Holland, it will be remembered, did not come into existence as an autonomous state before 1609. Until then, Dutch art had been inseparably linked with the general artistic activities in the Netherlands, but with the emergence of the United Provinces it underwent one of the richest developments in the history of Western art.

The acceptance of Protestantism meant the virtual end of official religious painting, since churches were now largely undecorated. Mythological and allegorical pictures demanded a type of classical education less common among Dutch patrons than in Southern Europe; and as a result, such subjects were less popular in Holland than in Italy and France. The well-to-do Dutch merchants wanted paintings of all that was most dear and most familiar to them—recognizable landscapes, still lifes, fondly executed genre scenes, and paintings of

3-12. *William II, Prince of Orange* (detail), by Anthony van Dyck

3-13. *Meleager and Atalanta,* by Jacob Jordaens

themselves and their families, their homes, their everyday activities, and even the streets through which they continually passed. It was, above all, in painting—and in painting the people and the natural world around them—that the Dutch excelled.

Moreover, their own Northern Renaissance provided an even richer background for such painting than the Italian Renaissance, with all its drama and excitement. Even when they were painting subjects from the Bible, the masters of the North depicted such episodes as quiet, homely scenes, often in contemporary costume and with everyday objects rendered in the most minute detail. We have spoken of Velázquez' and even Zurbarán's love of textural effects; yet these

artists could scarcely match the microscopic surface perfection of Jan van Eyck, who some two hundred years before Velázquez had succeeded in capturing, in his portrait of Giovanni Arnolfini and his bride, that very physical sense of depth which Velázquez captured in *Las Meninas* (Plate 2-14), and by much the same means: that of conveying the exact shade of color of the surface of objects, both in the foreground and at a distance, so that a convincing effect of the musty—but in places, sunlit—air of a room is achieved. It is likely that, in his meticulous recreation of reality, Velázquez was in fact influenced by the Northern masters, since Spain had politically dominated the Netherlands.

The intellectual ambitions of most seventeenth-century Dutch painters were modest. It was considered important that a picture should tell a story, or at least be highly descriptive, and that it should support the time-honored premise that, in the words of Aristotle, "man delights in imitation." With a lack of intellectual program, painting as pure craft became highly prized, as well as a basis of critical judgment. There were a great many artists, and to make a living at all, most painters had to specialize—not only in a class of subject but even in terms of composition types and detail. The result was that any formula which had been tried and found popular was repeated, with unwearying and unashamed competence. Be-cause the average Dutch painter took this practical, unromantic view of art, he was quite capable of giving up his profession if he got bored or if, which was more likely, some better-paying occupation was available. Even so distinguished an artist as Meindert Hobbema was prepared virtually to abandon painting after he became a wine-gauger for the Amsterdam authorities in 1668.

Genre paintings—usually consisting of an interior with figures—developed as the result of a number of influences. For one thing, the Dutch had a tradition of group portraiture; for another, there were to be remembered the great genre scenes of the elder Bruegel in the sixteenth century, even when

3-14. *Still Life,* by **Frans Snyders**

intended to illustrate proverbs or biblical narratives. The Dutch genre painters, however, might be divided into two groups. First, there were those who, like Adriaen van Ostade (1610–1685), wished to capture the spirit of Dutch life. These painters preferred scenes of conviviality, tavern interiors with figures drinking, fighting, and flirting (Plate 3-15). Of this type, Jan Steen (1626–1679) was perhaps the most brilliant. Steen, at all times cheerful and sentimental, could create works such as his *Tavern Scene* (Plate 3-16), crowded with figures, very much in the manner of Bruegel.

The second group consisted of those who concentrated on effects of light and texture, that is, on the visible, tactile reality of things which was so important to the artists of the North. Among these were Gerard Terborch (1617–1681), Pieter de Hooch (1629–after 1684), and notably Jan Vermeer (1632–

3-15. *A Country Quarrel,* by Adriaen van Ostade

3-16. *A Tavern Scene,* by Jan Steen

3-17. *Boy Picking Fleas off a Dog,*
by Gerard Terborch

1675). These painters' best compositions frequently included only one person or a few people, usually shown in repose in an uncluttered setting—a room or sometimes a courtyard. They chose to portray not the tavern world of Steen but rather views of upper middle class domestic life. Although the interiors they painted were not palaces, they were comfortable, even luxurious, dwellings; and their occupants were well dressed and often waited upon by servants. In fact, they re-created, in almost snapshot form, the daily life in the very homes where their pictures, like small mirrors, were meant to hang.

Like mirrors, too, these paintings reflected the surface appearance of reality. Terborch's *Boy Picking Fleas off a Dog* (Plate 3-17) shows his sitter at work on a very real and fluffy pet, which wears an expression of recognizable annoyance. Terborch was especially talented at painting the surface aspect of fabric, and in his *Lady Washing Her Hands* (Plate 3-18), the texture of the subject's satin dress, contrasted with that of the rug covering the table behind her, is a miracle of replication with paint on canvas. In the backyard of De Hooch's *Country House* (Plate 3-19), an equally recognizable scene is taking place. A man and a woman are enjoying a pipe and refreshments in the garden of what appears to be a two-family house. The brick of the back wall of the house, worn away at the edge of the roof, is depicted to perfection, while the entire group looks as it might be glimpsed by a passer-by.

The master who brought such genre painting to the level of great art was Vermeer, who, like De Hooch, was from Delft. Vermeer has inspired a great deal of fanciful criticism—"fanciful" because he is a thoroughly mysterious character, about whom very little is known. His life is poorly documented. He was apparently an art dealer and, judging from the number

3-18. *Lady Washing Her Hands,*
by Gerard Terborch

3-19. *The Country House,* by Pieter de Hooch

of pictures still in the possession of his family after his death, did not depend for a living on selling his work. He appears to have painted very few pictures and upon his death was deeply in debt.

But if he was, in this sense, something of an amateur, he was decidedly an amateur of genius. He pinned down on canvas the effects of light and texture accurately, and with a faultless sense of tone. Thus Vermeer could create illusions on canvas that have—without any loss of descriptive accuracy—an almost abstract beauty of their own. Like Velázquez, he succeeded in "painting the air." In his work entitled *The Painter in His Studio* (Plate 3-20), Vermeer caught,

with photographic precision, the look of a slightly creased parchment map hanging against a flat wall. But in painting the tufted hanging rug that is pulled to one side in the foreground, Vermeer has gone beyond what the camera can reproduce. So perfectly has Vermeer captured the impression of light absorbed and dulled by the soft surface of the rug that it is hard for the viewer to realize he cannot touch it by merely putting forward his hand. There is, moreover, a complete sense of the third dimension: to a spectator, the figures are actually located behind the drapery and well within the room.

As one can see in his painting *The Little*

3-20. *The Painter in His Studio,* by Jan Vermeer

Street (Plate 3-21), Vermeer was as great a master as De Hooch at portraying the warm red brick of Dutch architecture. Here he depicted with equal perfection the grubby whitewash at street level and the threatening heaviness of the cloudy skies.

In his *Woman at a Window* (Plate 3-22), Vermeer contrasts the warm, heavy wool of a rug with the hard, metallic glitter of a brass pitcher and basin. Both this painting and his *Young Woman Reading a Letter* (Plate 3-23), one of the greatest of his works, are triumphs of simply posed composition. The balance of color tones is nearly perfect, and in both works he has caught the exact effect of sunlight filtered through a thick-paned window.

Vermeer had, however, one limitation as an artist. His figures are quietly posed but somewhat lacking in life. Not one looks as if it might suddenly spring into action. Vermeer painted objects, and he painted light itself—the most difficult feat of all for the artist; yet he did not paint living and breathing people. In a way, although all his known works do contain figures, they are in reality supreme examples of still life.

Gabriel Metsu (1629–1667) was one of a group of Dutch painters who worked in an anecdotal vein of genre. He created interiors of quiet domesticity, with their occupants going about everyday tasks, as well as more crowded and active scenes of street life in the city (Plate 3-24).

Still life as an independent form of art came into its own in the seventeenth century, and nowhere more successfully than in Holland. This may be because of the Dutch love of surface texture in painting, and it may also be because the new independence of Holland was based on material wealth, which might account for a love of paintings that concentrated on depicting material objects.

3-21. *The Little Street,* by Jan Vermeer

There were many favorite variations of the still life. There were the hunting still life, with its dogs and dead game, and the "Vanitas" (Vanity) still life, with skulls nestling among bric-a-brac, in a reference to human mortality. (A still life, even though lacking figures, was not necessarily meant to be a work without a moral lesson.) There were the so-called "breakfast pieces," with food set on a table; there were the still lifes featuring fish and the straightforward studies of flowers in a vase, which included carefully rendered drops of water and crawling insects to add to the conviction of lovingly observed reality. Certain details, such as a half-peeled lemon with its rind hanging down, seen in the *Still Life with Fruit* (Plate 3-25) by Jan Davidsz. de Heem (1606–1684), or a goblet partially filled with liquid (thus producing all sorts of distorted

3-22. *Woman at a Window,* by Jan Vermeer

3-23. *Young Woman Reading a Letter,* by Jan Vermeer

3-24. *The Vegetable Market in Amsterdam,* by Gabriel Metsu

3-25. *Still Life with Fruit.* by Jan Davidsz. de Heem

reflections and refractions of light), would occur repeatedly in an artist's work. A fine example of this last device is the *Breakfast Table* (Plate 3-26) by Willem Claesz. de Heda (1593/94?–1682). Here the inclusion of an elaborate watch was probably intended as a piece of "Vanitas" symbolism, stressing the passage of time and the folly of vanity.

Dutch seventeenth-century landscape had its roots in the sixteenth-century tradition. For example, a delightful artist of the early seventeenth century, Hendrick Avercamp (1585–1634), silhouetted his stiff, doll-like figures on sheets of crisp ice in the manner of Pieter Bruegel (Plate 3-27).

One of the major problems facing Dutch landscapists was that Holland is, topographically, a dull country. The great flat plains do not provide the most interesting and varied subject matter for landscape art. Artists learned how to emphasize the excitement of the sky and how to rearrange imaginatively and dramatize existing features, such as the magnificently twisted tree trunks in the *Landscape with Two Oaks* (Plate 3-28) by Jan van Goyen (1596–1656). Although Van Goyen's early works were crowded compositions, monochrome in color, he later came to prefer a simpler design, usually with a low horizon, and adopted a larger range of colors, so that the composition was created—rather than by overly important color contrasts—by the subtle relationship of dark and light areas. This "monochrome" technique was also adopted by Hercules Seghers (1589/90–c. 1633), whose paintings and etchings (Plates 3-29, 3-30) were much admired by Rembrandt.

A quite different form of landscape popular in seventeenth-century Holland was the "Italianate view," a curious mixture, evolved mainly by Jan Both (c. 1618–1652) and Nicolaes Berchem (1620–1683), both of whom had been in Italy, where they came under the influence of Claude Lorrain, the French painter of "classical" landscape living in Rome. Both and Berchem took their highly poetic, artificial compositions and strong, sun-drenched Mediterranean lighting from Claude's style, but they removed its most conspicuously foreign characteristics (Plates 3-31, 3-32). The craggy "southern" landscapes of Both and Berchem are filled not with nymphs or the gods and goddesses of classical mythology, but with contemporary peasants, travelers, and brigands. These pictures combined the robustness of Dutch genre painting with the habitual longing of a northern people for the warmth of the southern sun.

The most cunning, and in many respects the most able, of these painters of the "Italianate view" was Aelbert Cuyp (1620–1691). Cuyp began in the late 1630's as a painter in the manner of Van Goyen; but under the influence of Both and Berchem, he turned to a more artificial style, which combined in a more obvious way than his rivals specifically Dutch motifs—cattle, milkmaids, architectural details—with a Mediterranean atmosphere (Plate 3-33).

Unquestionably the finest of the Dutch landscape painters, who encompassed in his style the best of each technique, was Jacob van Ruisdael (1628/29–1682). Ruisdael was born in Haarlem, the son of Isaak Jacobsz. van Ruisdael and the nephew of Salomon van Ruisdael, both landscape painters. His uncle was particularly well known as a realistic, and often "monochromatic," painter. Ruisdael produced a great number of pictures, which are very varied in character (Plates 3-34 to 3-36). Many of his early works were straightforward views of pictur-

3-26. *Breakfast Table,* by Willem Claesz. de Heda

3-27. *Winter Landscape,* by Hendrick Avercamp

3-28. *Landscape with Two Oaks,*
by Jan van Goyen

esque sites, some of which can in actuality
be located today.   His later works, however,
are more artificially constructed and much
more dramatic.   He was surprisingly brilliant at imaginary scenes of mountainous
landscapes with torrents and waterfalls,
which he could never have seen, since, except
for one excursion across the German border,
he never left Holland.   Ruisdael's greatness
as a landscape painter lay in his ability to
bring out the stress and drama of nature,

3-29. *River in a Valley,* by Hercules Seghers

3-30. *Landscape,* by Hercules Seghers

3-31. *Italian Landscape,* by Jan Both

3-32. *Italian Landscape,* by Nicolaes Berchem

without ever losing sight of actual appearances. He owed a great deal to the pioneering work of his Dutch predecessors. He and the other painters of his generation learned from the monochromatic landscapists how to harmonize all the natural tones into a balanced composition, and this knowledge enabled them to reintroduce local color without losing a unified effect.

The Jewish Cemetery (Plate 3-37) is one of Ruisdael's most remarkable achievements. It combines, to an unusual degree, his ability to portray scenes with accurate realism—the treatment of the trees, for example, or of the rainbow and sky—and certain allegorical overtones. The scene is meant to be the Jewish burial ground at Ouderkerk, near Amsterdam. It is known, from contemporary drawings, that the site actually differed considerably in appearance.

Ruisdael was not a literary man, and we do not know the exact meaning that should

3-33. *Landscape with Shepherds and Cows,* by Aelbert Cuyp

3-34. *Woodland,* by Jacob van Ruisdael

3-35. *Landscape near Muiderberg,*
by Jacob van Ruisdael

3-36. *The Big Waterfall,* by Jacob van Ruisdael

be placed on his extremely personal interpretation of the scene. But two basic ideas seem to be contrasted. The first is the decay of human endeavor, as symbolized in the tombs and the ruined church on the hill. In this respect, the painting is like a "Vanitas" still-life. Against this image of decay, however, Ruisdael sets up a counter-image of fruitful nature, evident in the suggested movement of clouds, in the rainbow, in the leafy trees, and in the rushing torrent, a symbol of natural power of which the artist was particularly fond and often painted. Goethe, who knew *The Jewish Cemetery* well, stresses the cheerful character of the scene. Writing in 1813, he noted "the light about to conquer the rain squall."

Ruisdael's most successful pupil was the extremely talented Meindert Hobbema (1638–1709). Hobbema frequently imitated his master so closely that their works have been confused. Unlike Ruisdael, however, Hobbema did not instinctively see nature in dramatic terms, with stormy skies and rushing waterfalls, and he came to prefer a more placid, more restricted range of

3-37. *The Jewish Cemetery,* by Jacob van Ruisdael

3-38. *The Water Mill,* by Meindert Hobbema

3-39. *Calm Sea,* by Jan van de Cappelle

subject matter than his master. He specialized in woodland scenes, in which a clearing, a winding path, or a water mill (Plate 3-38) acts as the focal point of the composition.

As we have seen, there was hardly a single aspect of his environment that the seventeenth-century Dutch artist did not want to record. Moreover, for each aspect of life there were specialists, ready to satisfy this taste, though at the same time enhancing and slightly altering the actual facts. They painted not only landscapes but seascapes and townscapes as well. But, in reality, no sea was ever so calm as that on which the stately vessels of Jan van de Cappelle (c. 1624/25–1679; Plate 3-39) gently rode; no street quite so neat and clean as Jan van der

Heyden (1637–1712; Plate 3-40) would have one believe; and no church interior quite so austere as those depicted by Pieter Saenredam (1597–1665; Plate 3-41) or Emanuel de Witte (c. 1617–1692; Plate 3-42).

Portraiture was of course tremendously important, and of the many portrait painters active in seventeenth-century Holland by far the most brilliant—though not the most deeply feeling and perceptive with respect to character delineation—was Frans Hals (1580/85–1666). Although born in Antwerp, of Flemish parents, Hals lived for most of his life in Haarlem. He was popular and successful and much in demand, but his circumstances were never particularly fortunate, for he had many children and was always in debt.

Hals's earliest works have not been preserved, but in the first dated paintings now extant he revealed an amazingly assured technique. His painting *Young Couple in a Landscape* (Plate 3-43) may be a portrait of himself and his wife. At a glance, the cheerful and wholesome charm of the couple is convincingly painted, down to the last detail; yet, when one looks closely, one sees that the heavy black silks and taffetas they are wearing have been rather cleverly suggested with bold strokes of the brush. Hals soon learned, as Velázquez was to discover a few years later, that a naturalistic effect depends not on quantities of detail, meticulously rendered, but on creating an "impression" in accordance with the spectator's visual experience. Very early in his career, he appreciated the fact that an impression of drapery or skin, is more effective than a painstaking, fold-by-fold account.

Hals's "impressionistic" technique is more showily brilliant than that of Velázquez, and his effects are more lively. His large group portraits of militia members, such as his

Meeting of the Officers of the Militia Company of St. Hadrian in Haarlem (Plate 1-2), which we have already discussed, have an air of robust good humor and parade-ground swagger. Group portraits were very popular in Holland and were a particularly difficult task for the artist, because it was necessary to give each figure relative prominence, and the results were often stiff and wooden. Hals was expert at breathing life into these works and composing a group to appear as if casually presented in the midst of action, while at the same time giving each figure individual importance.

Apart from group portraits, which after the disbanding of the military companies in 1648 (with the Peace of Münster) were generally devoted to the governing bodies of charitable institutions, Hals painted individual portraits and genre sketches, such as his *Portrait of Willem Croes* and *The Bohemian Girl* (Plates 3-44, 3-45). In these his free, "impressionist" style is seen at its very best. With a very few strokes of the brush, Hals has captured the vital, momentary expression of his subjects. Hals's output was extremely large, and it is likely that he was assisted, especially in the genre pieces, by members of his family. Still, in his old age, he was beset by poverty. In these later years, the free gaiety of his earlier manner gave way to a much more serious understanding of human character. His works began to resemble, in some ways, those of his great contemporary Rembrandt van Rijn (1606–1669).

To understand Rembrandt, one must be aware that a Caravaggesque movement had reached Holland by this time. Painters such as Hendrick Terbrugghen (1587/88–1629; Plate 3-46) had gone to Italy and returned much impressed by the shadowy and dramatic effects of Caravaggio. Another of this

3-40. *Nyenrode Castle,* by Jan van der Heyden

3-41. *Interior of the Church of St. Adolph at Assendelft,* by Pieter Saenredam

3-42. *Interior of a Gothic Church,* by Emanuel de Witte

3-43. *Young Couple in a Landscape,* by Frans Hals

group of painters, centered in Utrecht, was Pieter Lastman (1583–1633), with whom Rembrandt himself studied.

Rembrandt's name might well be placed beside that of Rubens, Velázquez, Caravaggio, or the greatest masters of the High Renaissance in the pantheon of painters. His earlier work shows the influence, the surface perfection, of the other Dutch painters of his day, and also that of Caravaggio; but Rembrandt went beyond his countrymen to become one of the greatest baroque painters—and beyond even the glorious baroque tradition to become, in his deep compassion and understanding of the tragic element in human life, one of the greatest of all painters.

Rembrandt's exact position in art is perhaps best expressed by Sir Kenneth Clark in his book *Rembrandt and the Italian Renaissance:*

In the year 1620, when the youthful Rembrandt went to the University of Leyden, Dutch painting might have seemed, to the outside observer, to be profoundly and almost incurably provincial. A Dutch patron looked to one or the other of the schools for the kind of painting he required: modest, complacent portraiture, detailed still life (with, as often as not, a moral attached), and quasi-topographical landscape. The more cultivated patrons recognized that great art existed beyond their borders in Venice, Rome and Bologna, and even in Flanders, where, since 1610, the fame of Rubens had been established; and they applauded those of their countrymen who had been bold enough to attempt an international style, especially the Utrecht painters Honthorst and Terbrugghen, who had learned the exciting new tricks of Caravaggio. They also praised, though with less conviction, the attempts of an Amsterdam painter, Pieter Lastman, to practise the kind of historical painting by which, according to the theorists, art could become respectable. But in their attempt to

3-45. *The Bohemian Girl,* by Frans Hals

push their local painting into the mainstream of traditional art, Dutch connoisseurs were hampered, as the English were hampered two hundred years later, by the convictions of a protestant, democratic community. The Church could no longer patronize art directly.... State patronage, without the willful taste of an individual autocrat, was as half-hearted then as it is today. It is true that the newly rich bourgeoisie were keen to form collections, but their taste in contemporary paintings was not of a kind to change the domestic character of Dutch art. Looking at the scene in 1620 an intelligent critic might have predicted a Jan Steen or a Hobbema; but he could hardly have imagined that one of his countrymen might achieve the peculiar greatness of a Titian or a Donatello, that quality which Matthew Arnold called "high seriousness," and which, in the art of painting, seemed to be reserved for those brought up in a tradition of monumental religious art, with its roots in Mediterranean antiquity.

This miracle took place; it was achieved by Rembrandt. . . .[1]

Born the son of a prosperous miller, Rembrandt went to the University of Leiden before he undertook the serious study of painting with several masters, including Lastman. He opened his studio first in 1625 in Leiden and then moved to Amsterdam in 1631 or 1632, by which time he was quite well known. In 1634 he married Saskia van Uylenborch, who brought with her a sizable dowry, and Rembrandt lived lavishly, buying magnificent clothing, luxurious furnishings for his home, and fine paintings by the

[1] Sir Kenneth Clark, *Rembrandt and the Italian Renaissance*, New York University Press, New York, 1966.

3-46. *The Duet,*
by Hendrick Terbrugghen

3-47. *Self-portrait with Saskia,* by Rembrandt van Rijn

3-48. *Stormy Landscape,* by Rembrandt van Rijn

masters he admired. Moreover, he was enjoying tremendous success as a portrait painter. Rembrandt was particularly gifted with just those talents which the Dutch admired most—the ability to capture a brilliant likeness of his sitters and to describe to perfection in paint their furs and velvets. His portraits of this period have a superbly smooth and jewellike finish, and in his *Self-portrait with Saskia* (Plate 3-47) Rembrandt is seen in a joyful moment before the shadows gathered around his life.

Rembrandt was already far more than the usual Dutch portrait painter, however. Working in a variety of media, he considered drawing and etching as important as painting. He was also expert at nature studies

3-49. *Portrait of the Artist's Son Titus,* by Rembrandt van Rijn

111

3-50. *The Night Watch* (detail), by Rembrandt van Rijn

and at landscape. In this latter form he was an admirer of the painter Hercules Seghers, several of whose works he owned, and he himself painted marvelously imaginative views, such as his *Stormy Landscape* (Plate 3-48), in his distinctive warm golden tones. Moreover, Rembrandt's art changed. Unlike so many of his Dutch contemporaries, he had a great interest in man's moral history, and he painted scenes from mythology and above all from the Bible, at times using friends and even his family as models.

It was in 1642 that Rembrandt's life took a tragic turn. In that year his wife, whom he adored and often painted, died. She had borne Rembrandt several children, but only their son Titus lived to adulthood (Plate 3-49). The same year Rembrandt painted his great group portrait of the militia company of Captain Frans Banning Cocq, traditionally known as *The Night Watch* (Plate 3-50). The company is depicted at the moment of being called to arms, and there is a great sense of preparation and movement. Some figures shuffle about in shadow, while others are pinpointed by rays of uneven light. As a painting, it is far greater than Hals's *Meeting of the Officers of the Militia Company of St. Hadrian in Haarlem* (Plate 1-2), but as a group portrait it was rather unfair in the attention given to some of the sitters.

For whatever reasons, Rembrandt now ceased to be in demand as a fashionable

3-51. *The Supper at Emmaus,* by Rembrandt van Rijn

3-52. *Flora* (detail), by Rembrandt van Rijn

painter, and his public deserted him. Rembrandt, depressed by his wife's death, became less and less interested in the kind of bright, expensively upholstered portraiture which was then in favor and which he had been prepared to supply in the past. The seemingly haphazard brushstrokes of his increasingly free style were directly opposed to the highly polished surface technique that was so marked a feature of Dutch painting. He is said to have become difficult in personal relations and unaccommodating with clients, and his style became more and more puzzling. Rembrandt now turned more seriously to the painting of religious and symbolic subjects. These he created not for any patron but for his own satisfaction.

Like his Dutch contemporaries, Rembrandt wanted to record his actual environment; where he differs is in his extraordinary capacity to transform his material. Hals, Steen, Terborch, and Vermeer were artists of great technical proficiency, but their minds and concerns were fundamentally commonplace. They observed their portrait sitters and studio models, chairs, and brick walls and set these down with all the skill and accuracy at their command. But Rembrandt had the most vivid of imaginations, and he looked more deeply into reality. For instance, among the homeless Jews who were exiled by the Spanish Inquisition and who had taken refuge in Amsterdam, he found the faces he felt must have been like those of the personages of the Bible. He also realized that men are in all generations the same; only their circumstances differ, and so his woebegone, but elaborately dressed models all befitted scenes set in other times and places, but situations in which humanity is ever, eternally the same. In Rembrandt's shadowy interiors, are seen faces stamped with the tragedy of life—and, once seen, are never forgotten. His painting of a New

Testament episode, *The Supper at Emmaus* (Plate 3-51), is such a work, although, true to the simplicity of Christ's teachings, the setting is not a lavish one. Similarly affecting is his painting entitled *Flora* (Plate 3-52). In his declining years, spent in constant struggle against poverty, Rembrandt took his devoted housekeeper, Hendrickje Stoffels, to live with him and often used her as a model. In this work the housekeeper, dressed in a flowered hat, is meant to represent the goddess of spring; but her aged and still beautiful face bears no promise of springtime, only a look of world-weary and eternal sadness.

By 1656 Rembrandt declared bankruptcy. He sold his house, furnishings, and art collection and moved to lodgings in the poor Jewish quarter of Amsterdam. Still, although he was no longer anywhere near the center of taste, Rembrandt continued to exercise an almost hypnotic influence over his contemporaries. His style of the 1620's and 1630's remained popular throughout the next three decades. He was brought in for the decoration of the new Amsterdam town hall in the early 1660's, and the guild of drapers asked him to paint their group portrait, which he completed in 1662. To these last commissions, as in his *Family Group* (Plate 3-53), dated as late as 1667, he brought all the depth of human understanding he had acquired over many years of suffering. When he died in 1669, he had already buried his only surviving son.

The great flowering of Dutch art occurred in the seventeenth century, and during the eighteenth century there were few outstanding painters. It was in the eighteenth century, however, that Germany, which had been culturally as well as physically devastated during the Thirty Years' War (1618–1648), regained some of her former

3-53. *Family Group,* by Rembrandt van Rijn

energy and produced works of artistic merit, though these were strongly influenced by styles from other countries.

In the first decades of the eighteenth century, Italian influence dominated German painting. Italian prestige in this field continued to be high throughout the century, and in 1750 Tiepolo himself was summoned from Italy by the Prince Bishop of Franconia in order to decorate the Palace of Würzburg. The Italian master was paid 30,000 florins, as against the 1,000 florins that Melchior Steidl and Johann Zick, local artists, received for similar work.

Tiepolo's masterpiece, however, had less effect than might have been expected, for by 1730 a wave of French influence had spread throughout Germany and Austria. The solidity of Italian baroque was replaced by a lighter, more delicate rococo style, which owed much to the French painter Antoine Watteau and to the immense prestige of the French court at Versailles.

The origins of the rococo style are French, as we have seen, and for these one must go back to the decorative patternbook engravings of Jean Bérain in the 1680's. His designs consisted of fine curling tendrils of linear "arabesque," which owed something to the delicately painted wall decoration of the Golden House of Nero, discovered in the sixteenth century, and also to the abstract, scroll-like decoration of the baroque. The possibilities and variations of the arabesque were further explored by other designers in France in the last years of the seventeenth century and at the beginning of the eighteenth. Artists such as Antoine Watteau produced many delicate and intricate designs that were then used as part of interior decorative schemes.

But this graceful style, in turn, gave way to a graver, more sober one in the second half of the eighteenth century. This was due, in part, to a new kind of French influence, but it is far more a reflection of increasing admiration for Dutch painting. Dutch artists had always been renowned for landscape and genre subjects. With the rise in importance of the middle classes toward the end of the century, these forms became more important in the German states.

But, with few exceptions, it was not in painting or sculpture but in the field of architecture and interior decoration that the artists of Germany and Hapsburg Austria showed particular excellence. There is an underlying unity in the architecture of Germany and Austria in the eighteenth century—a unity that belies the political structure of the two countries. Though Austria gained in strength and confidence as a state after the defeat of the Turks outside the walls of Vienna in 1683, Germany was not a single country but an agglomeration of about 300 separate city-states, principalities, and bishoprics. It is true that Germany and Austria still formed the basis of the Holy Roman Empire, but Voltaire correctly, if caustically, noted that in the eighteenth century it was "neither Holy, nor Roman, nor an Empire."

Despite their political differences, a consistent architectural style spread throughout the two countries. This was largely based

3-54. Abbey Church, Rottenbuch (near Munich)

on the late Italian baroque movement derived, originally, from Bernini and Borromini. The French style of Versailles and the more recent French rococo also affected German and Austrian architecture. Basically, it could be said that church architecture, particularly in Austria and the Catholic states in Germany, derived from Italian sources, whereas the palaces for the aristocrats of both countries were designed after the French fashion. So it was that, during the eighteenth century, baroque and rococo buildings were constructed at the same time in Germany and Austria. Still, notwithstanding the influence of France and Italy, German architects and the painters, sculptors, and stucco artists who created architectural decoration managed to go beyond their models and create works that were quite original and immensely charming.

The late baroque style perfectly suited the

Roman Catholicism of Austria and many German states, where memory of the struggle between Catholics and Protestants in the religious wars of the sixteenth and seventeenth centuries was still fresh and the Catholic Counter Reformation was still in progress. The emotional force of the churches of eighteenth-century Germany is conveyed directly to the visual sense. The Bavarian has been called a "man of the eye," and the same could be said of all Germans who responded to the baroque architecture of the period. The worshiper was made to feel that the interior of the church was a vision, on earth, of the divine bliss of heaven, and German baroque interiors were freer, lighter, and gayer than anything that had been seen before.

The Abbey Church of Rottenbuch (Plate 3-54) is an example of how decoration can completely transform an interior. The medieval structure of the church was given a "face-lift" with stucco and frescoes covering all available wall and ceiling space. However, it can also be seen that, whereas the decoration of Rottenbuch is obviously applied (that is, added as an afterthought), in churches designed by Johann Michael Fischer (1691–1766), such as the Benedictine Abbey of Zwiefalten (Plate 3-55), or the great interior of the Church of the Fourteen Saints (Vierzehnheiligen), near Bamberg, by Balthasar Neumann (1687–1753; Plates 3-56, 3-57), architecture and decoration have been conceived as a unified whole.

The art of the German and Austrian courts was founded in this extraordinary political situation of Germany in the eighteenth century. The 300 or more separate states of which eighteenth-century Germany was comprised were governed by virtually independent rulers, who ranged from the Emperor of Austria through electoral, spiritual, and lay princes, counts, and prelates, down to officials who were little more than country squires. The only real semblance of unity was to be found in Hapsburg possessions such as Bohemia, Moravia, Silesia, and the Tyrol, which made Austria still indisputably the greatest of the Germanic powers. Some of the other notable German states included Bavaria, with Munich as its capital; Saxony, having Dresden and Leipzig as its principal towns; Brunswick-Lüneburg, with Hanover as its capital; and such ecclesiastical territories as Mainz, Cologne, and Trier (Treves).

3-55. Benedictine Abbey, Zwiefalten, by Johann Michael Fischer

3-56.   Church of the Fourteen Saints, near Bamberg,
by Balthasar Neumann

In spite of the aura of magnificence with which the rulers endowed themselves, their sources of income were usually severely limited, as was the scope for expansion and development within their domain; hence, to a large extent, they were content to devote themselves to the pursuit of pleasure and to the exercise of absolute power.

To impose a pattern on the various elements that made up court life, the princes invented a formulary of etiquette, based on Versailles but supplemented by local and often ridiculous practices, prescribing everything from the number of horses to be harnessed to a carriage to the number of pages for attending a prince, and so on. Only electors (those princes who participated in the selection of the emperor) used large forks and knives and sat in red velvet chairs, as distinct from guests, who sat on green velvet. Such ceremony and artificial restraints were probably welcomed as a support in a bored and leisurely society.

A great many of the rulers, however, were sincere and hard-working men, who, even if unspectacular, did manage the affairs of

their lands with quiet efficiency; and a few of them were destined to make substantial contributions to the history or culture of their country.   Such a man was the Elector of Bavaria, Maximilian Emanuel II.   From 1692 to 1701, he was stadtholder (viceroy) in the Spanish Netherlands and, after siding with France against Austria in the war of the Spanish succession, spent some ten years in exile.   On his return to Munich in 1714, he immediately turned his attention to architecture and, together with the many artists and craftsmen he had brought back, started to put into operation ideas he had picked up during his years of exile spent near Paris, thereby establishing in Bavaria a strain of rococo art some ten years before it appeared anywhere else in Germany.

In terms of architecture, rococo meant simpler, more restrained lines in the general structure, without the flaring bulges of the baroque style, and plane surfaces delicately decorated with finely chiseled arabesques and other sculptural detail.

At Nymphenburg, three miles from Munich, Maximilian Emanuel II continued work on his summer palace, a structure dating from 1663 that had been extended and remodeled between 1702 and 1704. Originally consisting of the plain central block, it was enlarged by the addition of two-storied galleries and twin lateral pavilions.   After 1715, work was continued under the Elector's protégé Joseph Effner (1685–1745), and the great ballroom of the central block was extended upward through three floors.   Its vault (Plate 3-58), decorated with stucco and fresco in a fashion more baroque than rococo by J. B. Zimmermann (1680–1758), has as its subject an allegorical representation of the advantages of rule under the electoral family and shows the goddess Flora as she accepts a bouquet of flowers from a nymph—"the Castle of the

3-59. The Pagodenburg, Nymphenburg Park, by Joseph Effner

3-57. Interior, Church of the Fourteen Saints, by Balthasar Neumann

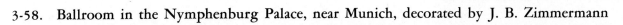
3-58. Ballroom in the Nymphenburg Palace, near Munich, decorated by J. B. Zimmermann

Nymph alone being worthy to be the summer seat of the noblest electoral Bavarian gods and goddesses and their nymphs," according to an inventory of 1758.

On the grounds of the Nymphenburg Palace, between 1716 and 1719, Effner built the Pagodenburg (Plates 3-59, 3-60), a tiny, two-storied octagonal pavilion with crossed extensions, which was used for entertaining. The kitchens were built in a separate block, out of sight, and food was served through the windows "in order that one should not be disturbed by the servants," according to Graf Preysing. The striking decoration of the lower, central room, incorporating blue-and-white Delft tiles, was doubtless influenced by Louis XIV's Trianon de Porcelaine on the grounds of Versailles. Upstairs, the decoration (Plate 3-61) displays the first example in Germany of *chinoiserie*, the Chinese-inspired fashion that had already established itself in France.[2]

A later room in the Nymphenburg Palace itself was designed by François de Cuvilliés (c. 1698–c. 1767), a deformed dwarf from Hainaut whom the Elector had trained as an architect, and whose genius is best seen in the Amalienburg (Plate 3-62). This

[2] The Far East, and China in particular, held a tremendous fascination for the sophisticated nobility and gentry of the eighteenth century. Accurate knowledge of Chinese customs and dress was transmitted to Europe largely through the engravings and paintings of a French Jesuit missionary, Father Attiret, who became court painter to the Emperor of China and died in Peking in 1768. The exotic dress and unusual architecture of this ancient civilization, which had for so long remained isolated from the West, provided wonderful source material for palace murals and tapestries.

3-60. **Room in the Pagodenburg, Nymphenburg Park**

3-61. Chinese Room in the Pagodenburg, Nymphenburg Park

small hunting pavilion, also on the grounds of the Nymphenburg Palace, was built by Cuvilliés between 1735 and 1739 for Amalia, the wife of the elector Charles Albert, who was Maximilian Emanuel's son. The main feature of the lodge, which is a fine example of rococo architecture, is a circular saloon, from the balcony of which the royal party would shoot the pheasants that were specially reared on the palace grounds. The mirrored room, the Salon des Glaces, which is exquisitely decorated with a series of mirrors set in a color scheme of blue and white, with stucco decoration overlaid with pure silver foil, is flanked on either side by a spacious suite of rooms. Provision was also made for the dogs in the *Hundekabinet.* The Amalienburg was frequently used as the scene of the *Wirtschaft,* a mock country fair strongly reminiscent of those held at the Trianon in Versailles—the constant model for all the lesser aristocracy of Europe.

3-62. The Amalienburg, Nymphenburg Park, by François de Cuvilliés

England

IN THE seventeenth century England enjoyed a brilliant age of architectural development, owing to the genius of two men: Inigo Jones (1573/76–1652) and Sir Christopher Wren (1632–1723). Although their works show many "baroque" details, neither could be called a distinctly baroque architect, that is, in the style of a Bernini or a Borromini. They chose instead to follow the earlier, simpler, and more severe style of the Italian High Renaissance.

Both men held the very widest interests. Apart from Jones's duties as an architect, for instance, he designed and stage-managed the masques, the elaborate verse and pantomine performances that formed so important a part of court entertainment.

4-1. Banqueting Hall, London, by Inigo Jones

His significance as an architect lies in the fact that he was the first man in England to apply Italian Renaissance principles of architectural form to the total design of a building. Elizabethan architects knew of the Italian sources through treatises and patternbooks, but they merely consulted these as storehouses of ornamental detail, which they would employ in a wholly decorative, surface manner on structures that were medieval in plan and proportion.

Inigo Jones, in buildings such as his Banqueting Hall in London (Plate 4-1), observed all the proper rules of proportion and considered the overall classical *harmony of form* to be as important as the classical *details,* in a design that freely uses the elements of Greek and Roman architecture as they had been interpreted by the architects of the Italian High Renaissance. To get some idea of Jones's break with traditional English architecture of the era, it is interesting to compare his Banqueting Hall with Hatfield House (Plate 4-2), built in the Elizabethan style earlier in the century, a project to which the young Inigo Jones had contributed "drawings of some Architecture" for the sum of £10.

Unfortunately, the number of Jones's buildings is very small, and what might have been his greatest work came to nothing. In the late 1630's plans were afoot to build a vast palace for Charles I along the same principles of design as those used in the Banqueting Hall, which would itself have been incorporated into a side of one of the courtyards; but with the outbreak of the Civil War (1642), this grandiose scheme was abandoned.

Christopher Wren began his extraordinary career at the age of fifteen, when he became an assistant demonstrator in anatomy at the College of Surgeons. During his stay at

Oxford, he took up science and became fascinated with problems of astronomy, physics, and engineering. It was not until the great fire which demolished a large section of London in 1666 that Wren, a member of the royal commission for rebuilding the city, took up architecture seriously.

He was chosen to design many of the new churches (no less than fifty-one within the city limits and four outside), as well as the new St. Paul's Cathedral (Plate 4-3). After the fire, St. Paul's was found to be in such dangerous condition that it had to be demolished. Wren was commissioned to design the new cathedral, which was begun in 1675 and finished by 1710. His main aim was to create not only a place of worship but also a great landmark that would dominate the city skyline—which indeed it did until the advent of the skyscraper. With this in mind, Wren concen-

trated all his attention on the dome with which he crowned his original, centralized plan. But this first scheme was abandoned in favor of a structure with a longitudinal nave. The final design has much of the grandeur of Michelangelo's St. Peter's, with the addition of baroque details, such as the elaborate treatment of the pediment over the two-tiered colonnades of the facade.

With his wide knowledge of French and Italian architectural design and with his experience in engineering problems, along with the experimental bent of his mind, it is hardly surprising that Wren should have brought to his designs an extraordinary variety of solutions. Nonetheless, he preferred a strict classical style, and works such as his Library of Trinity College in Cambridge (Plate 4-4), with its unrelenting arched colonnade, when seen across a broad expanse of English lawn, have a severe and

4-2. Hatfield House, Hertfordshire, by Robert Lyming

4-3. St. Paul's Cathedral, London, by Sir Christopher Wren

elegant grandeur not to be found elsewhere.

The finest achievements of English eighteenth-century architecture were the large country houses built throughout the British Isles. For over seventy years it seemed that both major and minor architects of England could do no wrong. But in England the architecture of the eighteenth century was no closer to French rococo than the architecture of the seventeenth century had been to baroque. English architects still chose to pattern themselves on the architects of the High Renaissance, and this was the time of the Palladian movement, largely created by Richard Boyle, Earl of Burlington, and his architect William Kent (1685–1748), both ardent admirers of Andrea Palladio, the renowned sixteenth-century Italian Veneto exponent of an outwardly academic style that often combined the elements of the classical orders with boldness and imagination, as well as rational organization of space. Burlington's publication of various works by Palladio did much to inform and convert a generation of architects. Through the publications of Burlington and the practical example of Kent in his Palladian buildings, English architects were provided with a system that required taste and judgment rather than original genius to produce, time and again, designs of great elegance.

The existing building of the Senate House in Cambridge (Plate 4-5) is only one wing of James Gibbs's (1682–1754) original and handsome Palladian plan, which was for a three-sided group of buildings. The design was not entirely by Gibbs, who was brought in to "make what improvement he shall think necessary" to a plan made by an amateur, Sir James Burroughs.

Born near Aberdeen, Gibbs studied in Holland and Italy, where he was a pupil of Carlo Fontana, himself a pupil of Bernini. On his return to England in 1709, he became a friend of Wren. His circular library in Oxford, the Radcliffe Camera (Plate 4-6), is yet another of his original and exciting designs, although its deliberately roughened ("rusticated") first story does not appear suited to bear the heavy dome and upper stories, which are bound into a single massive drum by the soaring two-story columns.

John Wood, Sr. (1704–1754), a Yorkshireman by birth, was working in Bath by 1725. One of a group of provincial architects to be attracted to the Palladian manner, he enjoyed, like Gainsborough, the opportunities provided by the most fashionable spa in England to create some of the finest work of his generation. In Prior Park, his most famous villa (Plate 4-7) and a typical example of the new English country residence, we see the gracious two-storied portico of Roman or Greek proportions so beautifully illustrated by Palladio.

But of all names connected with the Palladian movement, that of Robert Adam (1728–1792) is perhaps best known. He was one of four talented brothers from Scotland (the others being John, James, and William). Robert was the principal architect, James was also an architect of ability, and the other two brothers usually collaborated as business partners. Derby House in London (Plate 4-8) is not perhaps the most

4-4. **Library of Trinity College, Cambridge, by Sir Christopher Wren**

4-5. Senate House, Cambridge, by James Gibbs

4-7. Prior Park, Bath,
by John Wood, Sr.

4-6. Radcliffe Camera, Oxford,
by James Gibbs

famous of Robert Adam's buildings, but its handsome facade has typically lofty Palladian proportions.

One might say that authentically British painting began in the eighteenth century. As far as painting was concerned, the Italian Renaissance had been slow to cross the Channel. Even at the time that Charles I was acquiring his magnificent collection of Italian art, so-called "English painting" was largely the work of artists born and trained on the Continent. The King patronized foreign artists such as Rubens and employed Sir Anthony van Dyck as his court painter. It was Van Dyck who dominated English portrait painting until the Commonwealth.

During the Puritan reign of Cromwell and the Commonwealth, art very naturally went into a decline, but with the restoration of Charles II the situation rapidly improved. Charles II was never as seriously interested in art as his father had been and was apparently a man of much less sensitivity, but he had a liking for luxury and display that resulted in patronage for decorative fresco artists from the Continent.

Sir Peter Lely (1618–1680), who was appointed Charles II's principal court painter in 1661, was in great demand for his languid, sensuous portraits of the ladies of the court (Plate 4-9). Lely's style was based directly on Van Dyck's, but he lacked his great predecessor's refinement and nervous sensibility. All his female subjects appear with unvarying white skin, huge watery eyes, and rounded cheeks—the period's ideal of beauty. Whereas Van Dyck had created elegant and richly aristocratic portraits, Lely was showy in his technical proficiency and effects. But then it was, in many respects,

4-8.   Derby House, London, by Robert Adam

4-9. *Portrait of a Woman,* by Sir Peter Lely

a showy age. As a businesslike portrait artist, Lely thrived; and so did the German-born Sir Godfrey Kneller (1646/49–1723), a painter of dull, often pompous portraits, who rapidly became Lely's successor and dominated the scene until his death.

From 1715, when the Englishman James Thornhill, winning out against strong Italian competition, was awarded the commission for the decoration of the dome of St Paul's, to the death of Turner in 1851, England was a source of artistic activity that rivaled any other country in Europe.

The causes of this amazing development were connected with the equally startling growth of the British Empire's political and economic power. At a time when she was a dominant power in the world, it was increasingly felt to be wrong that Britain should be inferior to Europe in the "arts of elegance." It was to foster English art that the Royal Academy was founded in 1768—120 years after the French Academy. On the occasion of its opening, on January 2, 1769, its first president, Sir Joshua Reynolds, said: "It is indeed difficult to give any other reason why an empire like that of Britain should so long have wanted an ornament [the Academy] so suitable to its greatness, than that slow progression of things, which naturally makes elegance and refinement the last effect of opulence and power."

Unfortunately, those who felt most strongly about the inferiority of English painting were the painters themselves, who saw foreign artists such as Verrio and Laguerre prosper in England, while accomplished native artists were ignored. Even worse, many English patrons, having had their tastes formed by an Italian Grand Tour, preferred to spend their money on Old Masters, rather than on the often negligible works of their countrymen. It was hoped that the new Royal Academy would impose what the English called the "Great Style" (a general term for the baroque painting of Italy, France, and Spain and of Rubens in the Netherlands) upon the young school of English painting, and Sir Joshua Reynolds delivered annual discourses to the students in which he analyzed the style and advised them on how best to acquire it.

The Great Style had been the possession of the ancient Greeks and Romans, of Michelangelo, and, above all, of Raphael. It demanded a certain method of drawing and coloring according to a system of ideal proportions. Its highest expression was known as "history painting" in England. In this type of art, painters took noble and heroic subjects from history (which included mythology and the Bible) and sought to avoid an overemphasis on details of costume and characterization that might reduce the scene to mere anecdote. They also avoided effects of color and texture that appealed to the senses rather than to the intellect, in striving to give their paintings an ideal and universal aspect.

By the beginning of the eighteenth century, every artist outside Italy was aware that the Great Style was in decline. Reynolds hoped that, with the foundation of the Royal Academy, "the dignity of the dying art might be revived." Until the end of the century, however, the suspicion lingered that the Great Style could be achieved only by Continental painters, that it was a gift which had not been bestowed upon the English. Aristocratic patrons did not want history paintings executed by their own countrymen. Thus, in 1766, an admirer of Benjamin West's *Pylades and Orestes,* who nonetheless refused to buy the picture, said: "You surely would not have me hang up a modern English picture in my house unless it were a portrait." Reynolds himself admitted that he preferred the humble portraits of Gainsborough to the works of contemporary "graduates in the great historical style," and he added that "we have the sanction of mankind in preferring genius in a lower rank of art to feebleness and insipidity in the highest." Nevertheless, every ambitious English painter was haunted by the idea of the Great Style, which would ennoble his art and distinguish him from the "mere mechanick."

Meanwhile, for the majority of English painters, only one course was open. However uncertain or prejudiced were his tastes, an Englishman of sufficient wealth required that his likeness be painted. From the visit of Hans Holbein the Younger in the sixteenth century to the advent of Sir Godfrey Kneller, foreign artists had found a lucrative income, and often a title, by working as portrait artists in England. Thus, portrait painting became for the native painter not only the most profitable pursuit but also that craft most readily studied in the works of Rubens, Van Dyck, or other earlier masters.

Two men, namely, Sir Joshua Reynolds (1723–1792) and Sir Thomas Gainsborough (1727–1788), dominated portraiture and, consequently, English painting during the second half of the century. Rivals professionally, they have come to be identified as contraries, like the Carracci brothers and Caravaggio before them.

Reynolds, an emulator of Raphael and Michelangelo, friend of that great literary figure Samuel Johnson and of the parliamentarian Edmund Burke, exemplified the definition of painting as a learned profession, based on rules and principles. The first president of the Royal Academy, he was honored with knighthood and a doctorate of civil law at Oxford (at that time a unique distinction for a painter). He was also official painter to King George III.

Gainsborough was, on the other hand, a provincial by choice. He never visited Italy and was content to continue working in the fashionable resort of Bath long after achieving the reputation that made him one of the forty founding members of the Royal Academy. He received little official recognition in the way of honors (though he was the preferred painter of the royal family) and arrived, as Reynolds said, "to great fame, without the assistance of an academical education." He painted not according to rules but from his observation of nature.

Reynolds is most deservedly remembered as the first Englishman and the last European to formulate a theory of art and artistic education that was truly academic. His fifteen *Discourses,* delivered to the students of the Academy's classes, are sensitive and perceptive essays in art, his true memorial. His few attempts at compositions in the Great Style are unsuccessful; yet his portraits owe much of their effect to his ability to give them a "heroick" style. He painted Admiral Keppel in the pose of a classical statue, the *Apollo Belvedere,* and he painted the actress Mrs. Siddons as a Michelangelesque Tragic Muse, seated on a cloudy throne (Plate 4-10). Even in a painting such as his *Portrait of the Misses Waldegrave* (Plate 4-11), Reynolds managed to give a classical monumentality to the domestic occupations of embroidery and silk winding, and but for their powdered wigs and laces, the three ladies might well be goddesses or Muses.

It is ironic that the first president of the Royal Academy, who was professionally and personally dedicated to the ideals of Raphael and Michelangelo, should have found frequent employment and lasting reputation for works such as his *Portrait of Master Hare* (Plate 4-12), that is, for the portrayal of oversweet children. Nevertheless, these are often delightfully drawn and delicately colored with free, sweeping brushstrokes, and it is doubtful whether any painter has ever been more successful at capturing the soft charm of a child.

Still, Michelangelo remained Reynolds's ideal, and at the end he admitted: "I have taken another course, one more suited to my abilities, and to the taste of the times in which I live. Yet, however unequal I feel to that attempt, were I now to begin the world again, I would tread the steps of that great master."

Gainsborough, at the end of his life, also regretted the time spent on portraiture. He said that he wished to take his viola da

4-10. *Portrait of Mrs. Siddons as the Tragic Muse,* by Sir Joshua Reynolds

4-11. *Portrait of the Misses Waldegrave*, by Sir Joshua Reynolds

gamba and go off to some pleasant village where he could paint landscapes. Typically, he preferred the lowest to the highest accepted forms of painting. He painted several large compositions including peasants and gypsies, so-called "fancy pictures," such as his *Landscape with Connard Village* (Plate 4-13). In later life he often composed this sort of work from a handful of pebbles and twigs on the studio table; drawn as they were from his "fancy," they resembled Rubens's landscapes more than the Suffolk of Gainsborough's own boyhood.

Whatever his varied interests, it was as a portraitist that Gainsborough was best known. His early portraits, such as his *Conversation in the Park* (Plate 4-14), give only a slight hint of his mature style; yet, despite the awkwardness of his inexperienced technique, there is evident in the delicate coloring and light touch of Gainsborough's brush a rococo elegance that reminds the viewer of the French origin of Gainsborough's teacher, Hubert Gravelot.

Gainsborough's great works, often of women of the aristocracy, such as his *Portrait of Mrs. Graham* (Plate 4-15), are paintings that are stunning in their beauty. In them he captured all the excitement and magnificence of England at the height of its power. Unlike the girl in *Conversation in the Park,* Mrs. Graham is not docile, but is an alert and fascinating creature. Gainsborough's subjects, particularly his women, are not generalized types, like the large-eyed beauties of Lely, but are strongly characterized individuals, whom, despite their richly decorated clothing, he did not necessarily flatter. When he painted Mrs. Siddons (Plate 4-16), he made her a lady of fashion, rather than a Tragic Muse as Reynolds had, and dressed her in shimmering lace, with powdered hair and a large hat, the famous Gainsborough hat. He made no apparent attempt to idealize her character or features according to classical formulas. His complaint while working on her portrait became famous: "Confound the nose; there's no end to it."

Gainsborough was also capable of charming paintings of more intimate and simple subjects, such as his portrait of his daughters, Mary and Margaret (Plate 4-17). His paintings of children have all the charm of Reynold's works but are less idealized.

Apart from Reynolds and Gainsborough, there were other portraitists of genius in eighteenth-century England. George Romney (1734–1802), the rival of Reynolds and Gainsborough, is no longer considered their equal; yet in the best of his works, such as *Anne, Countess Albemarle, and Her Son* (Iveagh Collection, Kenwood House), he applies the principles of classical design far more attractively than Reynolds himself.

4-12. *Portrait of Master Hare,* by Sir Joshua Reynolds

4-13. *Landscape with Cornard Village,* by Sir Thomas Gainsborough

Alan Ramsay (1713–1784) and Sir Henry Raeburn (1756–1823) were two Scots who gained a national reputation. Ramsay was one of the few British artists of the period to be trained in Italy. In the field of the "grand manner" portrait, he proved a match for Reynolds and was appointed official painter to King George III, in preference to Reynolds, who had to wait his turn. Raeburn, who was an orphan, lacked professional training of any kind; yet he rose to knighthood and the position of king's limner (an illuminator or painter) for Scotland in 1822. His light good humor is evident in his portrait of the Reverend Robert Walker (Plate 4-18), posed in the act of skating, with his clerical garb outlined against the white of the ice.

Sir Thomas Lawrence (1769–1830) was a portrait draftsman at the age of ten. Among the many accomplishments of his enormously successful career, he was an associate of the Royal Academy at age twenty-two, and at twenty-three was appointed painter to the king after the death

4-14. *Conversation in the Park,* by Sir Thomas Gainsborough

4-15. *Portrait of Mrs. Graham,* by Sir Thomas Gainsborough

4-16. *Portrait of Mrs. Siddons,* by Sir Thomas Gainsborough

4-17. *Mary and Margaret, the Painter's Daughters,*
by Sir Thomas Gainsborough

4-18. *The Reverend Robert Walker Skating,*
by Sir Henry Raeburn

4-19. *Portrait of Miss Elizabeth Farren,*
by Sir Thomas Lawrence

136

of Reynolds. A full R.A. at twenty-five, he was later knighted and became president of the Academy in 1820. His best portraits have a stern, though somewhat empty dignity and are firmly, abeit mechanically, handled. Yet in works such as his *Portrait of Miss Elizabeth Farren* (Plate 4-19) the subject is far from stern, and Lawrence replaced dignity with pure impishness. Lawrence's finest serious work went into a series of large ceremonial portraits of those European statesmen who had opposed Napoleon, subjects that were well suited to his more dignified style. These were commissioned by the Prince Regent for the Waterloo Gallery at Windsor Castle.

The English aristocrats wanted not only portraits of themselves, their wives, and their children, but they also wanted portraits of their horses as well. This need was handsomely satisfied by George Stubbs (1724–1806). Stubbs, who was born in Liverpool and later studied anatomy in York, went to Rome to confirm for himself that "Nature was and always is superior to Art, whether Greek or Roman." His diligent study of nature led him to the most unattractive of self-imposed tasks. In a remote Lincolnshire farmhouse he performed his own dissections on the carcasses of horses, in order to produce the superb series of etchings entitled *The Anatomy of the Horse,* which was finally published in 1766.

Stubbs was frequently employed to make portraits of famous thoroughbreds, and it was as an animal painter that his reputation was established. Such paintings as *Molly Longlegs with a Jockey* (Plate 4-20) show that Stubbs was no mere horse painter, however, but an interpreter of the cool, hard lines of classical art, as well as a master of clean, simple composition.

Landscape and genre scenes were also considered suited to the English brush.

Richard Wilson (1713/14–1782) traveled to Rome and was influenced by the serene classical landscapes of Claude Lorrain. Upon his return, Wilson tried to bring this same serenity and warm light to his rearranged views of the English countryside (Plate 4-21), and he was strongly reproached by Reynolds in one of the *Discourses.* George Morland (1763–1804) specialized in rustic genre scenes, much in the spirit of the seventeenth-century Dutch painters. His paintings of country inns, peasants, cowherds, milkmaids, and fox hunts (Plate 4-22) enjoyed great popularity, and he provided his patrons with a view of humble life that was altogether pleasing, even if unrealistic. He painted these scenes in a rough, irregular technique that appealed to viewers bored with the smoother style of the great portraitists. (Morland, also, was one of the first English painters to sell his work through an agent rather than directly to clients.)

While the courts of Europe were always prime patrons of art, much Italian and Spanish art was created for the church, and therefore for the people at large. In Holland, artists painted to please middle class merchants and to decorate their homes. As we have seen, in England in the seventeenth and eighteenth centuries, art was created not for the church and, by and large, not for the court of the king, as had been so in France, but for the landed aristocrats and wealthier members of society who lived out their lives on country estates. In the early eighteenth century, the French writer Le Blanc observed: "One might almost say that luxury reigns as much in the country in England as it does in the cities in France. The English farmer is rich, and enjoys all the conveniences of life in abundance. In several parts of England a farmer's servant drinks his tea before he goes to plow."

Behind this prosperity lay a gradually changing social structure. The once numerous small farmers or squires were being steadily absorbed into the great estates of the nobility and the wealthier gentry, including successful merchants and professional men who were now moving out into the countryside.

The way of life on these large estates spread an impression of general elegance. Whereas in France and other countries the court had been the focal point of patronage, the English aristocracy had hundreds of artistic centers, spread over the country, rich in collections of pictures, furniture, books, and *objets d'art*. The enthusiasm of these numerous patrons perhaps more than compensated for lack of interest in art among the Hanoverian kings at the English court.

The sites of these country houses were chosen for their beauty, and the natural vistas were improved by inspired landscape gardening. The fashion was to conserve a natural look, relying on grass and trees, groves, streams, and winding walks, with an occasional temple or ruin as a concession to classical interest.

Many owners of country seats also had a house in London, to which they might come for business purposes or for the many pleasures to be enjoyed in the capital. The most elegant of the pleasure spots were perhaps the parks and gardens, especially Marylebone, Ranelagh, and Vauxhall. In these splendid settings, people would

4-20. *Molly Longlegs with a Jockey,* by George Stubbs

4-25. *Marriage à la Mode* (detail),
Scene I, by William Hogarth

age," that his works were "in the historical style," but of an "intermediate species of subject, which may be placed between the sublime and the grotesque." His pictures were not simply slices of life but were carefully conceived and composed inventions. He was not ignoring the grand manner; but like Gay in his *Beggar's Opera,* he was inverting it, introducing the "antihero" to painting.

Hogarth compared his pictures to plays, and the characters in them to actors performing in a dumbshow. The academic critics never accepted Hogarth as a history painter. Reynolds expressed regret for those few occasions when Hogarth "very imprudently or rather presumptiously, attempted the great historical style, for which his previous habits had by no means prepared him." Hogarth's genius, said Reynolds, had "been employed on low and confined subjects" and, therefore, "the praise which we give must be limited in its object."

Despite the foundation of the Royal Academy—the idea of which Hogarth had strenuously opposed—the Great Style was not to be revived. Still, for the eighteenth century, it was felt that great art did require a "great" subject, which was soon to be found in depictions of contemporary fears of heroism and, eventually, in the great republican causes of the end of this century —that is, in the American and French revolutions.

France

WHEN HENRY IV ascended the throne of France in 1589, he found his country shattered by civil war and the added stresses of religious conflict and foreign intervention. Having made peace with the rebels and established a policy of religious toleration by the Edict of Nantes in 1598, King Henry was then free to devote his energies to the salvation of his country's fortunes, which were at exceptionally low ebb. The principal reform measures were directed toward improving the financial position of the crown and increasing general prosperity among all classes by a revival of agriculture, trade, and industry. But the most effective steps were those taken to strengthen the power of the monarchy, so that by the time of Henry's assassination in 1610 France was once more ready to assume a position as a leading European power.

This position was threatened, however, by the incompetence of Henry's widow, Marie de Médicis, who was dominated by unscrupulous favorites. The situation was saved by the appearance of Cardinal Richelieu, who became chief minister for Louis XIII in 1624 and continued the centralizing policy of Henry IV. During the middle years of the century, France's power was finally consolidated; her struggle with Spain and the Holy Roman Empire ended, and internal dissension was crushed, notably the disruption caused by religious differences and the ambitions of the nobility. With the coming of age of Louis XIV, the Sun King, who ascended the throne as a child in 1643 and ruled for the rest of the century, there was a marked improvement in French fortunes. This was in part due to Louis's wise choice of chief minister in Jean Baptiste Colbert. Colbert's rigid and successful policy of centralization was not without effect on the arts, too, which in this period reflected the most complete state control perhaps ever exercized in artistic matters.

Colbert held that art should serve the glory of France and the king and, thus, should be organized and codified like any other branch of the state. Charles Lebrun (1619–1690) was found eminently suitable to direct this "department" of government, since he was versatile and talented and had demonstrated administrative capacities. This policy led to the foundation of the Gobelin works and the academies, that is, the various societies of learned and qualified men devoted to furthering the arts. The purpose of the Gobelin manufactory was to produce everything necessary for furnishing the royal palace of Versailles, and its development resulted in a high level of technical skill, if not great inventiveness. In 1648, moreover, an academy was set up for the theoretical organization of the visual arts, based on the assumption that the practice of art could be learned by the application of certain precepts. Thus, during this period there was an official doctrine concerning the arts which everyone accepted—had to accept, in fact, if they were ambitious, because all great commissions came from the crown.

It was above all an age of classicism, though not so much at the court. The French intellectuals' admiration for the literary and artistic works of the Greeks and the Romans, which exceeded even that of the Italians, can be seen as a sort of veneer on the baroque spirit of the age. The philosophers Descartes and Pascal thought along simple, classical lines of logic; Corneille wrote tragedies in masterful imitation of Greek and Roman drama; and in their paintings Nicolas Poussin (1594–1665) and Claude Lorrain (1600–1682) attempted to

5-1. House of the Caryatids, Dijon

put before the eyes of viewers the antique world in all its perfection. The greatest architect of the era, François Mansart (1598–1666), restrained the flourishes of the Italian baroque with a kind of grand classicism—perhaps because the art of the Italian Renaissance, with all its ardor for the recaptured beauties of Roman architecture, was at that time stressed in France, as it was in England.

In many ways, the most important developments in architecture in the early years of the seventeenth century were the result of Henry IV's plans for remaking the city of Paris. His projects included completion of the Pont Neuf, which had been begun in 1578, and the Place Dauphine and the Place Royale. Place Royale, now known as Place des Vosges, was begun in 1605, and its symmetrical disposition of modest-sized houses around a square was to prove important to the future development of town planning and influenced later schemes in Germany, the Netherlands, and England.

François Mansart, born in Paris, was the son of a master carpenter. His rise to fame was rapid, and by the mid-1630's he was working on the Château of Blois for the Duke of Orléans, brother of Louis XIII, as well as several townhouses in Paris for the rich financiers who were to form the most important part of his clientele. A comparison of Mansart's Château of Maisons-Lafitte with the earlier House of the Caryatids (Plates 5-1, 5-2), constructed in 1603 in Dijon, will give some idea of the strides made in architecture in France during the seventeenth century. Like the buildings of the Grand' Place in Brussels, the House of the Caryatids is random and medieval in structure and proportion, with classical sculpture merely as surface decoration on its façade. The design of the Château of Maisons-Lafitte is one of sweeping grandeur and handsomely balanced, classical proportions, and its decoration is restrained. It has the deeply pitched, double-sloped roof common to buildings of the period in France, and in it one sees the emerging form of the mansard roof, to which Mansart gave his name. It was only in the buildings he designed for the clergy, such as his Church of Val-de-Grâce (Plate 5-3; completed by Jacques Lemercier and modified by Le Muet), that Mansart and his contemporaries employed the ornamental, capricious lines and the elaborate decoration which typified the Italian baroque.

Louis le Vau (1612–1670) was a less grandly severe architect than Mansart, and his designs are on the whole more decorative. In some of his ingenious plans for Paris houses he reveals great skill in creating harmonious, classical effects despite extremely difficult sites. The most important of Le Vau's middle-period works was the Château of Vaux-le-Vicomte, which was commissioned by the financier Fouquet in

5-2. Château of Maisons-Lafitte, Seine-et-Oise, by François Mansart

1657. With its gardens by André Le Nôtre (1613–1700) and its very elaborate interior decoration (in part the work of Charles Lebrun), the mansion was to prove something of a trial run for the splendors of Versailles, Le Vau's greatest assignment.

At Versailles, outside Paris, Louis XIII had built a small château in 1624, which was in basic form a court surrounded by three wings. Louis XIV developed an early affection for the place and called in his chief architectural advisor Le Vau to make alterations. However, in 1669 Louis decided to go ahead with the architect's more radical scheme for enclosing the old château with a new building which concealed the garden side but which left intact the original interior façades of the wings fronting on this "Marble Courtyard" (Plate 5-4). Versailles was to be the center of Louis's ever-expanding universe, and its all-important garden façade is the most monumentally impressive in Europe (Plates 5-5, 5-6). As originally planned and executed by Le Vau, the ground floor had a rusticated base; the first story above was decorated with a row of Ionic

pilasters and columns, and the straight roof-line above was adorned with statues. Jules Hardouin Mansart (1646–1708), the immensely talented grandnephew of François Mansart, later filled in the terrace created by a receding area in the center of Le Vau's original plan and added sprawling wings on either side, these modifications giving the palace its present-day appearance. The whole shows an admirable grasp of the principles of classical architecture, combined with a feeling for grandiose scale. The effect is totally symmetrical, and the whirling fantasies of the Italian baroque are nowhere in evidence.

The splendor of the exterior depended, to a large extent, on its setting and especially to the gardens laid out by Le Nôtre during the 1660's. Nature was tamed and organized to conform with the dominant architectural note of symmetry: hedges were cut into regular shapes, parks laid out according to geometric designs, and the overflow of fountains and pools made to follow pre-arranged channels. The interior of the palace was even more splendid, a fit background for the numerous ceremonial occasions and the complexities of court life. The ceilings in the earliest of the surviving rooms are decorated with a mixture of stucco ornamentation and painted figural compositions. The walls in some rooms were covered with patterned crimson or green velvet, on which were hung Italian paintings from the royal collection. Other rooms were faced with varicolored marble panels arranged in classical rectilinear patterns. Floors were also paved with the same luxurious material, and the furniture consisted of elaborately inlaid tables and cabinets, and sometimes was wholly of silver. The grand staircase designed by Le Vau and decorated by Lebrun was the most spectacular of all the inventions at Versailles; it consisted of a short broad flight, which then divided into two flights following the long walls and which was lighted by an opening in the middle of the ceiling. This brilliant and novel design paved the way for the second stage in the creation of Versailles, in which Jules Hardouin Mansart replaced Le Vau as the chief architectural force.

The younger Mansart is responsible for several of the most handsome and richest

5-3. Church of Val-de-Grâce, Paris, by François Mansart (completed by Jacques Lemercier)

interiors of the palace, among these the room known as the Salon de la Paix and the splendid Galerie des Glaces (Plates 5-7, 5-8), the great mirrored hall that is perhaps the best-known room of any palace in the world. Begun in 1678, its barrel-vaulted ceiling was painted by Lebrun and his pupils with episodes from the life of Louis XIV.

5-4. "Marble Courtyard," Palace of Versailles

5-5. Eastern (Garden) Façade, Palace of Versailles, by Louis Le Vau and Jules Hardouin Mansart

Owing to the technical difficulties of making large sheets of glass, the mirrors are each composed of several panels, which are not precisely aligned, and the resulting distortion adds to the striking effect of the chamber.

Mansart was also responsible for the Grand Trianon (Plate 5-9), a large and luxurious pavilion constructed in the park of Versailles as a place of retreat, where the King could escape the court formality.

No account of the architectural evolution of Versailles would be complete without visualizing the brilliance and sumptuousness of court life as lived there under Louis XIV in the late seventeenth century. Far more than a great palace, it was a world in itself, a policy and a system of government, for one of Louis's subtle motives for building a palace large enough to accommodate the entire aristocracy was to crush its power by having all the nobles under his eyes as his permanent retinue. The Duc de Saint-Simon, one of the shrewdest chroniclers of life at Versailles, tells that the King "looked

to right and left, not only upon rising and upon going to bed, but at his meals, in passing through his apartments or his gardens, where alone his courtiers were allowed to follow him. He saw and noticed everybody: not one escaped him, not even those who hoped to remain unnoticed."

More intimidating than the personality of the King was the rigid system of etiquette which governed both King and courtiers down to the smallest details of daily life and which defined precisely the relation of each member to another.

The courtiers moved in phenomenal splendor; yet court life itself was strictly ordered, unvaried, and tiring. In winter the pleasures were comedies, concerts, balls, gambling, masquerades, and *appartments,* the evening receptions of the King, held once or twice a week. Saint-Simon described these as "assemblies of all the court in the Grand Salon from seven o'clock in the evening until ten, when the King sat down to supper, and after ten in one of the Salons at the end of

5-7. Salon de la Paix, Palace of Versailles,
by Jules Hardouin Mansart and Charles Lebrun

5-6. Detail of the Eastern Façade, Versailles,
by Louis Le Vau and Jules Hardouin Mansart

5-8. Galerie des Glaces, Palace of Versailles, by Jules Hardouin Mansart and Charles Lebrun

5-9. Grand Trianon, Park of Versailles, by Jules Hardouin Mansart

the Grand Gallery. First there was some music; then tables were placed all about for all kinds of gambling. . . ."

In summer there was leisurely cruising in gondolas on the canal, promenades in the Orangerie and in the gardens, and readings and concerts at the Trianon. At fixed times of the year, there were journeys to Compiègne and Marly-le-Roi, and to Fontainebleau, where tennis and stag hunting were new diversions. The daily routine included the *lever* ("awakening") and *coucher* (" puting-to-bed") of the King, the Mass, dinner and supper, the hunt or a promenade, play or reading; and all was so strictly ordered that both King and courtiers were meticulously punctual.

Meanwhile, there was great ferment in the field of art. France suddenly produced a number of painters of genius, working in a variety of styles. In general, they might be divided into two groups: the followers of the Caravaggio baroque, and those who were classicists.

Among the followers of the style of Caravaggio, Simon Vouet (1590–1649),

Georges de La Tour (1593–1652), and the Le Nain brothers were outstanding. Simon Vouet was born in Paris and trained by his father, the painter Laurent Vouet. In 1611, at the age of 21, he accompanied the French ambassador to Constantinople. After that he went to Italy, arriving first in Venice and then going on to Rome, which remained the center of his activities until his return to France in 1627. In 1624, Vouet was elected president of the Roman Academy of St. Luke, which suggests the high esteem in which he was held by his fellow artists in the Italian capital.

During the early part of his Roman period, Vouet was much influenced by Caravaggio, and the French artist produced pictures such as *St. Bruno Receiving the Rules of the Order* (Plate 5-10), full of Caravaggesque sweep and drama. (St. Bruno was the founder of the Carthusian order.)

On his return to Paris in 1627 Vouet was an immediate success. He painted a series of altarpieces for several Parisian churches, as well as mythological and allegorical compositions and decorative schemes for various houses in the city. Most of these projects, which were very influential in their day, have disappeared; but a much-restored series of pictures, dating from about 1635–1640, can still be seen in the Arsenal in Paris. As the years passed, Vouet's style veered away from the influence of Caravaggio and became more classical in feeling, cooler in tone; his chiaroscuro (light-dark contrasts) was less emphatic, and his compositions were clearer and simpler. A good example of this later style is his *Allegory of Riches* (Plate 5-11), painted some four years before his death.

Georges de La Tour was an altogether curious figure. Very little is known about him, though it has been established that he was patronized mainly by bourgeois circles in Nancy and Lunéville, where he was settled by 1620. Nothing is known about his training, but it is possible that he acquired the Caravaggesque style in Utrecht. La Tour's earlier works have daylight settings and particularly bright, clear color. It is interesting to compare his *Fortuneteller* (Plate 5-12) with Caravaggio's treatment of the same subject (Plate 1-7). La Tour's is an eerie picture: the shriveled gypsy seer is a particularly wierd and frightening image, while the young man and his companion show a haughty distrust. It is also interesting to note La Tour's treatment of flesh; the faces of his figures, with the exception of the aged gypsy, have a smooth, masklike appearance.

In his mature years, under the influence of Caravaggio's style, La Tour invariably portrayed scenes in an artificial aura of night lighting, with figures of greatly simplified contour and poetic beauty, often dimly seen by the light of a candle: for example, his *Magdalen* (Plate 5-13).

Perhaps the most interesting examples of the Caravaggesque tendencies are to be found in the work of the Le Nain brothers. The pictures themselves—with their muted, limited color, their air of quiet, grave dignity, and their lack of dramatic or monumental effects—seem very different from the works of Caravaggio or his immediate circle. At the same time, it is hard to believe that the Le Nain brothers would have been moved to dwell on their humble models were it not for Caravaggio's example.

There were three Le Nain brothers: Antoine (c. 1588–1648), Louis (c. 1593–1648), and Mathieu (c. 1607–1677). All three were born at Laon in Picardy. Since nothing is known about their artistic training, their work has been the subject of a great deal of speculation. (The signed paintings bear only the surname, and the brothers are also known to have collabo-

5-10. *St. Bruno Receiving the Rules of the Order,* by Simon Vouet

5-11. *Allegory of Riches,* by Simon Vouet

5-12. *The Fortuneteller,* by Georges de La Tour

5-13. *The Magdalen,* by Georges de La Tour

rated.) It is sufficient to note that there are three distinct groups of paintings, to each of which the name of one brother has been convincingly assigned.

Louis Le Nain had settled in Paris by 1630. His paintings are larger in scale than those of Antoine, and their coloring is more subdued. He favored a range of grays and grayish-toned browns and greens. Although he occasionally produced religious and mythological pictures, most of his works are scenes of peasant life. Unlike most Dutch and Flemish painters of peasant genre scenes, he does not present jolly views of tavern life; his treatment is restrained and dignified. Paintings such as *The Peasant Repast* and *The Forge* (Plates 5-14, 5-15) are straightforward portrayals of the poverty of the French peasant in all its grimness. The wine they drink would hardly appear to warm their chilled feet. The early works of Velázquez are serious in this way; but Velázquez, as ever, was more concerned with

5-14. *The Peasant Repast,* by Louis Le Nain

pastoral landscapes in which the figures may seem incidental—which they were not. For Poussin at least the figures were much more central. Both tried to recapture what was thought of as the beautiful, tranquil world of antiquity.

With the passage of time, Poussin has become an artist who is increasingly difficult to appreciate fully. This is not because he was deliberately obscure but because many of the things he took for granted—in particular, a familiarity with classical mythology and the precepts of ancient philosophy—are no longer common knowledge. Poussin

5-15. *The Forge,* by Louis Le Nain

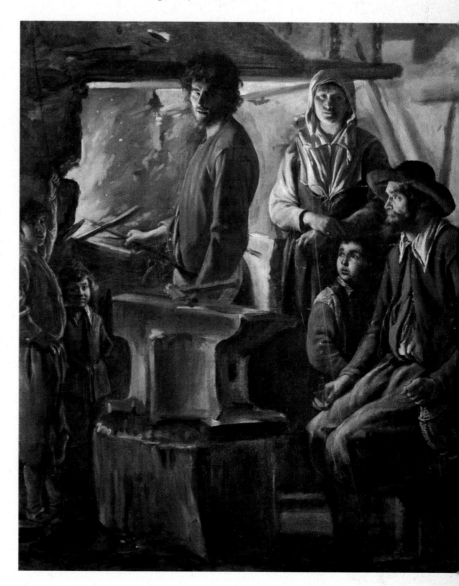

surface texture than with strong social comment. The world painted by Louis Le Nain was far removed from the gilded life of Versailles; and while his artistic comment on the state of France may have been observed, it was little heeded.

It is not surprising that intellectual patrons preferred to be wafted into the classical world of Nicolas Poussin (1593/94–1665) and Claude Lorrain (1600–1682). For most of their adult lives, both painters lived and worked in Rome and have as much right to be regarded as products of the Italian school as they do of the French. Both were highly successful in their day. By the 1640's Claude was internationally famous, with Pope Urban VII and King Philip IV of Spain numbered among his clients. Poussin moved in learned circles and was able to attract a highly discriminating clientele. Both artists preferred to work on a more modest scale and were not at their best in creating large canvases. Both often painted

5-16. *Landscape with the Woman of Megara Gathering the Ashes of Phocion,* by Nicolas Poussin

was an erudite artist, steeped in classical literature and the works of classical sculpture, and some reference to these was inevitably introduced in his paintings. Recognizing these reflections of the ancient world, whether in the form of a pose borrowed from antique sculpture or an illustration of a classical myth, is crucial to any genuine understanding of his work.

This passionate concern with the classical past of Greece and Rome recurs like a dominant theme throughout the French art of this period. Although it now presents a serious barrier to a thoroughgoing appreciation of the seventeenth century, antiquity was something very real to an artist like Poussin. For him, it was an ideal world that satisfied both his intellect and his emotions. The temples he introduced into his pictures, the mythological figures in classical dress, the myths and historic moments themselves, such as the life of the Athenian general Phocion, as taken from Plutarch, or the story of Orpheus and Eurydice, were all a part of this world which had survived in a tantalizing fragmentary form. Manuscripts of classical literature, the ruins of Rome, and broken statuary, urns, and pottery all became the object of endless study.

Poussin was born in Normandy of peasant stock; and after having worked with various painters in Paris, he left for Rome in 1624. He remained there the rest of his life, except for an unhappy return visit to Paris in 1640–1642 to work on the decoration of the Long Gallery in the Louvre, a large-scale undertaking that was unsuited to his slow, reflective working methods.

Poussin's earlier pictures were painted in warm tones and displayed a rather pagan gaiety, for the French painter had chosen Titian as his model. Later he fell under the influence of Raphael; his drawing became sharper, his color cooler, and the overall mood more austere. In paintings such as his *Landscape with the Woman of Megara Gathering the Ashes of Phocion* (Plate 5-16), Poussin has subjected the natural forms of trees and rocks to the same stringently controlled geometric formality as the architectural details.

The languorous figures in his painting *Inspiration of the Poet* (Plate 5-17)—the poet is represented as being instructed by Apollo, the god of poetry, who is portrayed with his laurel wreath and his lyre and attended by a muse—have the hard, smooth outlines of classical statuary, despite the rich color of the painting.

Claude's pictures are as concerned with the classical and biblical past as are those of Poussin. When their landscapes are compared, however, one can see that the character of Claude's work is very different. It is, for one thing, more natural. Notwithstanding his concern with philosophy and morality and human predicaments, Poussin could be remarkably indifferent to the appearance of the real world itself. The light in his landscapes is never quite convinc-ing, and the trees never look as if they grow in earth; whereas Claude based his equally artificial visions on a strict, perceptive observation of nature.

Claude made hundreds of drawings of the countryside around Rome. Many of these are no more than summary sketches, often done in bister (dark brown pigment prepared from wood soot) and wash, of a patch of trees or a group of rocks. These direct and constant links with nature, and in particular his preoccupation with effects of light, were important inasmuch as they helped Claude to make his artificially devised settings perenially fresh and vivid.

Claude Gellée, called Claude Lorrain because of his birthplace in French Lorraine, was first trained as a pastry cook but soon took up painting. In 1627 he settled in Rome, where he lived until his death in 1682. Until the mid-1630's, he painted small decorative landscape frescoes as well as canvases, but after that time he devoted himself exclusively to easel pictures. He achieved rapid fame and, by the second half of the 1630's, had emerged as the most notable landscape painter in Italy. It was at this time that he began to keep the *Liber Veritatis* ("Book of Truth"), now in the British Museum, a careful record of his paintings made primarily as a guard against forgery—which had already occurred as early as 1634.

Claude planned many works in pairs and, in these, paid careful attention to unifying elements such as corresponding masses and horizon line. In *The Marriage of Isaac and Rebecca* (Plate 5-18), for example, the picture is closed, as it were, on the right by a great clump of trees. The companion painting, *The Embarkation of the Queen of Sheba* (Plate 5-19), in which he brilliantly portrayed the optical effect of light on water, is closed on the left by a ruined classical building that

5-17. *The Inspiration of the Poet,* by Nicolas Poussin

reaches to the top of this evocative canvas.

It was formerly thought that Claude's figures were unnecessary or irrelevant—especially since they tend to be badly drawn—but this is far from the case. Many of the landscapes were intended to evoke the Arcadian world of classical myth, a world in which man lived in harmony with nature, on the abundant fruits of the earth; thus, far from being unimportant, Claude's figures are an integral part of the painting's meaning.

After the reorganization of 1663, the French Academy in Paris was, in reality, little more than an instrument of official policy, and for many years its director remained Charles Lebrun. Lebrun had worked in Rome, where he had studied both Italian baroque art and the work of Poussin, and after his return to France in 1646 succeeded Vouet as the leading painter of decorative schemes.

Lebrun received his first royal commission in 1661. Colbert was well disposed toward him, and Lebrun gradually took over every important post in the arts. He conceived much of the decoration for Versailles and was responsible not only for the painted elements but also for the design of statuary for the park and of the tapestries.

As director of the Academy, Lebrun advocated a strict adherence to the principles of Poussin, but in his own works he was much freer, as can be seen in his painting *Chancellor Séguier Surrounded by Attendants* (Plate 5-20). This difference was partly because the grandiose, decorative nature of his work demanded that visual points be made with greater force and emphasis than would have been possible were Poussin's style to be followed to the letter.

The academicians failed to take into account, however, the fact that the greatest series of masterpieces long on display in Paris was the cycle portraying the life of Marie de Médicis (Plate 3-3) by Rubens, a painter who, with his soft flesh tones and rich coloring, provided a model very different from Poussin. The controversy between the "Poussinists" and the "Rubenists" raged in the Academy toward the end of the century, and it was the warm, sensual style of Rubens that inspired artists of the next century.

By the first half of the eighteenth century, the character of French painting had become distinctly frivolous, both in its themes and their treatment. It was an art of luxury and coquetry, in which even the gods of Olympus descended to the parks of the great châteaux. Its lightness, elegance, and gaiety are in such contrast to the weighty drama and dignity of baroque art that it has been recognized as a distinct style, called rococo.

The new style seemed entirely appropriate for the times. In the reaction to the pomp and rigid ceremony of Versailles that followed the death of Louis XIV in 1715, court society moved to the elegant apartments of Paris. Under the regency of Philip of Orléans and, later, under the patronage of Louis XV's mistress, Madame de Pompadour, the arts became an inseparable part of the aristocratic life of ease and pleasure.

The first, and unquestionably the greatest, of the rococo painters was Jean Antoine Watteau (1684–1721). Born in Valenciennes, a Flemish town that had at that time become French, he went to Paris in 1702. After two years Watteau became a pupil of Claude Gillot, a minor artist who specialized in scenes from the theater, and by 1708 he was an assistant to a decorative artist, Claude Audran. His designs of this time—small, elegant figures and monkeys playing among trellises, festoons, and feathery arabesques—were already completely rococo in style.

It was probably while working with

5-18. *The Marriage of Isaac and Rebecca,* by Claude Lorrain

5-19. *The Embarkation of the Queen of Sheba,* by Claude Lorrain

Audran, who was keeper of the Luxembourg Palace, that Watteau saw Rubens's Médicis cycle, which had great effect on his later work. But at no time does Watteau appear to have tried directly to imitate Rubens. His earliest works were small military scenes in the style of the minor Flemish painters. He seems to have discovered his distinctive subject matter shortly after 1712, the year he was accepted as an associate of the Academy. He should have submitted a "diploma work" at the time of his acceptance, but he delayed five years before presenting *The Embarkation for Cythera* (Plate 5-21).[1]

The Academy honored him by inventing a new category for his work and accepted him as a painter of *fêtes galantes*. Watteau's *fêtes galantes,* small works that often contain many figures painted in minute detail, show a rich and leisured society idling on the terraces and in the parks of great estates (Plates 5-22, 5-23). Though they show similarities to earlier Dutch and Flemish paintings, they are substantially Watteau's own invention. The silk-clad figures—silk is Watteau's favorite material—drift through their opulent surroundings.

These small works are certainly not scenes of contemporary society. The clothes the characters wear, which to today's viewers seem so typical of the period, are in actuality a fancy-dress mixture in which costumes of different times and from the stage mingle with contemporary styles. Watteau compiled his finished works from albums of studies, some made from life and others taken from paintings, which he used over and over again. The world he depicts is an idyllic fantasy, redolent with memories

5-20. *Chancellor Séguier Surrounded by Attendants,* by Charles Lebrun

of Rubens and Titian, and even of contemporary fashion plates. But his fantasy is made into something touching by the realistic characterization of its inhabitants. They appear rather desolate, lost in the opulent land of make-believe that their riches have built around them. There is a certain melancholy that pervades all of Watteau's works.

Watteau often painted scenes and characters from the theater; yet, looking at his *Portrait of Gilles* or his *Mezzetin* (Plates 5-24, 5-25), both characters taken from the French and Italian comedies, it is difficult to tell whether the sadness they convey is that of the actor or the character he plays.

Watteau died of consumption at the age of thirty-seven, and perhaps the growing melancholy of his work was the result of his illness. Rubens had been able to create, in the Médicis cycle, scenes in which the

___

[1] It should be noted that an alternate interpretation holds that this painting depicts the embarkation *from* Cythera, that is, the departure on the return voyage from the island of love, the legendary birthplace of Venus.

5-21. *The Embarkation for Cythera,* by Antoine Watteau

5-22. *Conversation in the Open,* by Antoine Watteau

historical figures of Marie de Médicis and Henry IV moved among the gods of Olympus as if they themselves were gods. Watteau's mortals somehow seem to have attempted to enter the enchanted land of art, but for them the spell is broken—they are all too real. His followers, such as Nicolas Lancret (1690–1743), failed to grasp this special mood and saw in his inventions simply a land of delightful dreams, which they also attempted to portray (Plate 5-26).

As can be seen in his *Portrait of the Sculptor Antoine Pater* (Plate 5-27), Watteau was also a talented portraitist, far more serious in his approach than was Jean Marc Nattier (1685–1766), one of the principal portrait painters of the period. Nattier was much influenced by Rubens, and since he began his career by engraving that master's Médicis cycle, this is not surprising. In Nattier's work the strength of Rubens has become sweetness, his sweeping grandeur mere elegance. His portrait of the Marquise d'Antin (Plate 5-28), decorated with posies and attended by a lap dog and a pet parrot, reveals a typical ideal of the age.

5-23. *Fête Venetienne,* by Antoine Watteau

5-25. *Mezzetin,*
by Antoine Watteau

5-24. *Portrait of Gilles,* by Antoine Watteau

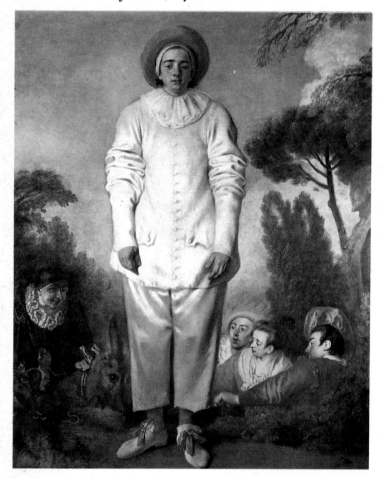

5-26. *Spring,* by Nicholas Lancret

The rococo style, with its delicately handled soft colors, was well suited to the pastel portrait, which had become the vogue in Paris through the works of the Venetian woman artist Rosalba Carriera. Two genuinely outstanding artists worked in this medium, Maurice Quentin de La Tour (1704–1788) and the Swiss Jean Étienne Liotard (1702–1789). Quentin de La Tour especially was a brilliant draftsman, as can be seen in the way he observed the sharp and quizzical features of his own face (Plate 5-29). Liotard's *Girl with a Cup of Chocolate* (Plate 5-30), a clearly drawn portrait of a serving girl, is a delightful piece of realism, as is his *Portrait of the Countess of Coventry* (Plate 5-31). Both are in certain details surprising for the age. The Oriental flavor of the Countess' portrait recalls Liotard's visit to Constantinople, following which he adopted Turkish dress and a beard, a manner that was oddly contrary to the simplicity of his style. But his appearance probably attracted valuable attention. When he

5-27. *Portrait of the Sculptor Antoine Pater,* by Antoine Watteau

visited England, Liotard had a great success, despite Horace Walpole's comment that his portraits were "too like to please."

The most successful and highly regarded painter of the generation after Watteau was François Boucher (1703–1770). At the age of twenty he was awarded the Prix de Rome; at thirty-one he was made a member of the Academy, and shortly after, through the influence of Madame de Pompadour, he became director of the Gobelin manufactory. Next he was made First Painter to the King (again through personal influence), and eventually he became director of the Academy.

It is ironic that Boucher's career should have so closely followed the course of the career of Charles Lebrun, leader of the Poussin adherents in the previous century, for few artists have treated tradition in so cavalier a fashion. He began his artistic education by engraving after the manner of Watteau, but he soon turned to Rubens for a style that he exercised with the same negligent ease as his nymphs wore their garments, for he regarded painting as a virtuoso performance.

In addition to mythological subjects, Boucher painted portraits, genre scenes, comical decorations, and picturesque landscapes. He also designed a series of tapestries in the Chinese manner, which were presented to the Emperor of China by Louis XV in 1764. Boucher might be described as a master confectioner. His paintings are charming fictions, unrelated to serious matters and admirably suited to the society that patronized him.

The goddesses of classical mythology had been popular subjects among artists for three

5-28. *Marquise d'Antin,* by Jean Marc Nattier

centuries before Boucher painted his versions of two favorite themes, the huntress Diana bathing and *The Toilet of Venus* (Plate 5-32). Rubens, in particular, had painted innumerable canvases with these subjects. But Boucher's pretty creatures are of a different race from the goddesses of Rubens. The nakedness of a Venus by Rubens seems natural; indeed, it is difficult to imagine her clothed. But the delicate flesh of Boucher's Venus could never endure any exposure to the open air. Moreover, though perfectly painted, his figures seem figments of the imagination, almost mechanically produced. Boucher, it is known, seldom used a model. After visiting him, Sir Joshua Reynolds reported with horror, "He said when he was young, studying his art, he found it necessary to use models; but he had left them off for many years."

Boucher's *Village of Issé* (Plate 5-33) was painted as a design for a stage set for the opera *Issé,* a drama with a pastoral setting. Boucher painted landscapes as easily and as prettily as he did figures. In an age when decorative "prettiness" counted for more than beauty, Boucher was a master.

The one outstanding exception to this universal taste for highly polished, overly elaborate, and delicately colored sweetness is to be seen in the work of Jean Baptiste Siméon Chardin (1699–1779), who was almost an exact contemporary of Boucher. No two artists could have been less alike, however, for Chardin was a painter of modest still lifes and sober domestic interiors, although his subject matter did not prevent him from receiving recognition even among Boucher's patrons.

Chardin first attracted attention in 1728 by exhibiting several of his works in an anteroom at the Academy alongside those of other painters. The Academy director, Largillière, noticed his painting of a rayfish

5-29. *Self-portrait,* by Maurice Quentin de La Tour

and thought it was by a talented Flemish painter. Chardin was accepted into the Academy in that same year as a genre painter of animals and fruit.

In the following years his still lifes and the scenes of daily life he had begun to paint attracted the attention of many collectors. In the form of engravings, his genre scenes also reached a wide public. By 1740, when he was presented to Louis XV (who accepted two paintings for the royal collection), Chardin was copying his own work to meet the demand.

Chardin's still lifes, usually combinations of familiar household objects, such as his *Still Life with a Smoker's Box* (Plate 5-34), are often so simple as to be stark. Nor did he favor the pale pink, blue, and white of Boucher's pallette.

Chardin was particularly gifted at portraying children. His paintings *Boy with a Top* and *Girl with a Shuttlecock* (Plates 5-35, 5-36)

5-30. *Girl with a Cup of Chocolate,* by Jean Étienne Liotard

5-31. *Portrait of the Countess of Coventry,*
by Jean Étienne Liotard

were probably commissioned portraits. Still, these might be considered essentially genre scenes, or even still lifes. In both, the sitters are not posed self-consciously; nor do they attempt to engage the spectator's attention but are, instead, engrossed in some familiar childish occupation. Their activity is mental rather than physical, and outwardly the sitters are as still as the objects around them. It is perhaps Chardin's ability to render the sweetness of a child's face with the detached objectivity he applies to a jug that prevents these works from seeming to be merely popular sentimental themes.

But then again, Chardin was the exception of his day. It was the aimless elegance and superficial existence of society as portrayed by Nattier and Boucher that truly reflected life at Versailles under Louis XV. It was still a splendid round of ordered entertainment, but without the force of Louis XIV's personality to give it genuine focus.

Culturally, France was the center of the universe. The French language itself was the common European language of diplo-

5-32. *The Toilet of Venus,* by François Boucher

industry were neglected, since by living at court the nobles lost interest in their distant estates. Abroad, the country suffered reverses of fortune. France damaged her reputation by the change of allegiance in the Seven Years' War, supporting her old enemy Austria against her ally Prussia; moreover, she lost her power in India and China and her position as a leading European political force.

The career of the King's favorite, Madame de Pompadour, exemplifies the peculiar combination of genuine taste and a love of art with foolish extravagance that epitomizes the age.

She was a well-read woman of remarkable energy, scholarship, and fun. She loved to acquire a house, decorate and furnish it lavishly, and then move on to another. The Hermitage, a secluded building on the grounds of Versailles, was particularly memorable. Because she disliked the dazzling decorations of the palace, Madame de Pompadour made the interior of this retreat deliberately rustic and simple. Here the king might often spend an entire day, while supposedly out hunting—occasionally, even cooking supper himself. The garden was filled with flowers, subtly arranged so as to lead from one delicious scent to another, and the plants were changed each day—just one example of her whimsical and fantastic extravagance in small things. Bellevue, the only large house she furnished, was sophisticated by contrast, one of the best examples of eighteenth-century French architecture. She commissioned Boucher, among others, to decorate it. The garden was a mass of china flowers from the Vincennes factory, which were perfumed to smell like real flowers and even deceived the king. She spared no cost in the furnishings, all of which revealed the perfection and exquisite detail of her taste.

macy and cultural exchange, favored for its logic and clarity. The superiority of French court art, cuisine, tapestries, furniture, and tableware was acknowledged, and these were eagerly sought after; French artists were given commissions by numerous foreign princes and kings. The architecture of Versailles itself was imitated in Germany, Austria, and Russia; and the popularity of French court life attracted noblemen, artists, and writers from the whole Continent.

Politically, however, the reign of Louis XV was unsuccessful, and the court had become but a shadow of its former self, for as a piece of governmental machinery devised by Louis XIV it was outworn, and his successor lacked the genius to modify it accordingly. At home, agriculture and

She was an exceptional patroness of the arts, both as a means to power and from genuine enthusiasm, and was fortunate in having almost an unlimited financial credit from the king. She loved china, which she both imported and acquired from the French factories at St. Cloud, Chantilly, and Vincennes. When the king gave her the village of Sèvres, she had the entire factory from Vincennes transferred to the village, where it prospered and attracted numerous artists and sculptors.

If anything, matters became worse under the well-meaning, but weak and ineffectual, Louis XVI, who understood little outside the art of hunting. Moreover, his Queen, Marie Antoinette, became very unpopular. The product of a diplomatic marriage be-tween Austria and France, she was surrounded by enemies at court from the start; she fed this hostility by her affection for intriguing favorites, which led her to interfere in public affairs. Her social extravagances gave further rise to scandal—in dress, jewelry, lavish balls, horse races, garden entertainments, and grandiose theatricals.

It was Marie Antoinette who was particularly fond of the Petit Trianon (Plate 5-37), the charming small pavilion built in the park of Versailles in 1762 by the most talented architect of the era, Ange Jacques Gabriel (1699–1782). Although an unmistakably rococo style of architecture took root in Germany in the middle of the eighteenth century, in France, where the style had developed in other arts, rococo exteriors were

5-33. *The Village of Issé,* by François Boucher

altogether exceptional, and rococo expression was almost entirely confined to interior decoration. The large private residences of the period, such as the Hôtel Matignon (Plate 5-38), designed earlier in the century by Jean Courtonne (1671–1739), were often built along lines of severe, almost unadorned elegance. The Petit Trianon itself is an extremely simple and beautifully proportioned square building, adorned by four Corinthian columns on one façade, balanced by four Corinthian pilasters on the other.

In the year 1761, two young men who were to be artists of importance in the generation after Boucher, set out for Italy together. Hubert Robert (1733–1808), then twenty-eight and later to become a curator of the Louvre, was a landscape artist who specialized in scenes in which ruined and overgrown architecture became the charmingly contrived setting for an idyllic rustic life. Often, as in *The Old Bridge* (Plate 5-39), he would place in a grandiose, theatrical setting the figures of washerwomen, who thereby became characters of romantic fantasy. Robert was much inspired by an outstanding French landscape artist of an earlier generation, Claude Joseph Vernet (1714–1789). Vernet often painted dramatic and sometimes frighteningly gloomy works, such as his *Embarkation for Cythera* (Plate 5-40), which show the influence of Salvator Rosa and Magnasco and do not at all remind one of Watteau. Like Claude Lorrain and Poussin before him, Vernet spent much of his life in Rome.

5-34. *Still Life with a Smoker's Box*, by Jean Baptiste Siméon Chardin

5-35. *Boy with a Top,* by Jean Baptiste Siméon Chardin

5-36. *Girl with a Shuttlecock,* by Jean Baptiste Siméon Chardin

5-37. Petit Trianon, Park of Versailles, by Ange Jacques Gabriel

Traveling with Robert was his friend Jean Honoré Fragonard (1732–1806). Trained by Chardin and Boucher, Fragonard won the Prix de Rome in 1752. Although he first attracted attention by painting in the grandest of grand manners, he soon developed a light, frivolous style inspired by Boucher and by Watteau's imitator Lancret. Like Boucher, he produced many kinds of pictures: portraits, picturesque genre scenes, and landscapes similar to those of his friend Robert. His painting *The Bathers* (Plate 5-41) is more frivolous than Boucher's own. Fragonard's work is more interesting technically, however, for he has painted his soft floating figures in a looser, almost "impressionist" style. This is even more true of his deliberately sketchy studies of washerwomen (Plate 5-42), which may bring to mind the similar late "impressionistic" works of Velázquez. Still, even these sketches have much of Fragonard's delicately decorative prettiness.

Fragonard often took themes from his

5-38. Hôtel Matignon, Paris, by Jean Courtonne

5-39. *The Old Bridge,* by Hubert Robert

5-40. *The Embarkation for Cythera,* by Claude Joseph Vernet

predecessors, ranging from Rembrandt to Boucher. In his *Blindman's Buff* (Plate 5-43), he has borrowed from Watteau, although painting with a broader technique. But by making no effort to characterize his decorative puppets, Fragonard excluded Watteau's human insight. Watteau had created his poignant spell by setting real people in the lost paradises of Titian and Rubens, but Fragonard won his reputation by removing from Watteau's art all such reality and melancholy. Yet Fragonard's charming figure, wandering blindfolded in a landscape of supernatural beauty, is a perfect symbol for the court of Versailles and the *ancien régime* (the "old order") for which it was painted. The blindfold would soon be removed, the charade ended.

The demand for reform had been gathering strength throughout the century. The court of France had been blind to the poverty and pathetic mismanagement of the country, or had seen it but had not realized that serious change was rapidly needed.

Meanwhile, the climate was one of revolution. The heart of the intellectual life of France in the eighteenth century was the world of the "salons," regular receptions held at the homes of certain hostesses, to which the wittiest, most learned men were invited to discourse on every imaginable topic. It was a unique achievement—but not surprisingly, a French one. One of the most regular and witty of salon attendants is said to have remarked, "The French are the most sociable people in the world, who talk more than they think, talk in order to think, and think only in order to talk." Such a national characteristic was as responsible for the vitality of the salons as was the personality of the successful hostess, who had to be particularly tactful, intelligent, and indefatigably interested in her guests. Historically, the salons not only reflected the great cultural activity of that period but also the freedom of speech and thought, and the rapid exchange of ideas which the private nature of the gatherings encouraged was

5-41. *The Bathers,* by Jean Honoré Fragonard

5-42. *Washerwomen*, by Jean Honoré Fragonard

partly responsible for the advanced notions set forth. Beliefs and institutions that had survived from the Middle Ages were challenged by a stream of ideas flowing from the philosophers, scientists, and writers of the age.

When François Marie Arouet, called Voltaire (1694–1778), fled to England to escape the tyranny of the French court, which had attempted to surpress his writings, he was amazed to discover a country with parliamentary government, religious toleration, a free press, no arbitrary taxes, and no imprisonment without trial. On his return to France, he became the spokesman for English rationalism and the central figure of the movement known as the Enlightenment, which sought to improve man and society by using human reason to abolish superstitious beliefs and conventions of the past and replace them with a rational system of knowledge. The literature of the Enlightenment, which culminated in the great Encyclopedia published in thirty-four volumes between 1751 and 1772, soon penetrated even the autocratic courts of Vienna, Madrid, and St. Petersburg.

It was now time for the court of France

5-43. *Blindman's Buff,* by Jean Honoré Fragonard

to face the new demand for freedom and equal rights, for the rule of reason to prevail. The famine year of 1789 brought the beginning of the end. It should be noted, however, that the initiators of the Revolution had originally aimed to limit the powers of the monarchy, not to abolish it entirely. The States-General (an assembly consisting of clergy, nobility, and the so-called "third estate") was called into session under heavy pressure from all three parties and, numerically, was dominated by the third estate, the populace at large. Because of the persistence of this last-named group, which swore not to disband until the constitution of the realm was set up and consolidated on firmer foundations, the three estates eventually amalgamated. Encouraged by the victory of the third estate, a Parisian mob stormed the prison of the Bastille, which seemed to symbolize monarchical tyranny. The incident was memorable, but not greatly effective. The national assembly of the three estates now quickly set about drawing up measures to abolish feudal vestiges and to safeguard human rights, while the King was in a conciliatory mood and while the mob was dangerously on the verge of losing patience. A procession of market women who marched on Versailles to insist on the King's acceptance of terms broke into the palace, nearly murdered the Queen, and escorted the royal family, followed by the assembly, back to Paris to take up residence in the Tuileries as virtual hostages.

Once the tide of rebellion had swelled, nothing could check it. Louis XVI and Marie Antoinette went to the guillotine, and along with them the inhabitants of Versailles: all those courtly beings who had danced, played, and banqueted, those who had doted on the works of Watteau, Boucher, and Fragonard—in effect, the entire world of the rococo.

5-44. *Bust of Madame Houdon,* by Jean Antoine Houdon

It is interesting to observe the spirit of the French Revolution as reflected in the works of probably the greatest artist of the era of Fragonard, the sculptor Jean Antoine Houdon (1741–1828). As can be seen in his portrait bust of his wife (Plate 5-44), he was capable of delicate works in the rococo style. Houdon could also create images of a more sober beauty, such as his shivering portrayal of *Winter* (Plate 5-45). *Diana* (Plate 5-46), considered one of his finest works, is a figure of the severest classicism, without soft prettiness or delicacy, but altogether noble and very different from the portrait of Madame de Pompadour as Venus (Plate 5-47) created a generation earlier by Étienne Maurice Falconet (1716–1791), a favorite sculptor during the reign of Louis XV.

5-46. *Diana,*
by Jean Antoine Houdon

5-45. *Winter,*
by Jean Antoine Houdon

It is not surprising that Houdon was responsible for the superb sculptural portrait of the seated Voltaire (Plate 5-48), in whose face one can see all the biting wit of the man most responsible for the French Revolution. Houdon's portrait of Benjamin Franklin is also very well known, and it is interesting to note that Houdon traveled to the United States in 1785 to portray George Washington for the state capitol in Richmond, Virginia.

Houdon was not alone as a classicist in this period. The Revolution prompted a return to the austere principles of the Roman Republic in dress, art, and architecture as well as sculpture. Forms of great republican sobriety, cool and hard in outline, took the place of the soft and playful figures of Boucher. In the wake of this revolutionary austerity, Fragonard died in 1806 in Paris, impoverished and totally forgotten.

The French Revolution was responsible for much more than a change of artistic style. It unseated, in art as well as in politics, the traditionalism and regard for the conventions of the past that had continued unquestioned for centuries, leaving a kind of unrest that in a sense has never since been resolved. Since 1800 artistic development has undergone many more fundamental changes than it did in the two hundred years preceding that date—a period in which the art of the Renaissance and of classical antiquity was spread throughout Europe and played upon in innumerable fascinating variations, like a musical theme.

5-47. *Madame de Pompadour as Venus,* by Étienne Maurice Falconet

5-48. *Voltaire Seated,* by Jean Antoine Houdon

ITALY

SPAIN

2-1. Clock Tower, Cathedral of Santiago de Compostela, by Domingo de Andrade.

2-2. *Pietà* (detail), by Gregorio Hernández. National Museum of Sculpture, Valladolid.

2-3. *Martyrdom of St. Bartholomew* (detail), by José Ribera. The Prado, Madrid.

2-4. *Drunken Silenus* (detail), by José Ribera. Capodimonte Museum, Naples.

2-5. *Jacob's Dream,* by José Ribera. The Prado, Madrid.

2-6. *Three Saints,* by Francisco de Zurbarán. National Gallery of Art, Washington, D.C. (Portrayed are SS. Jerome, Paola, and Eustachia.)

2-7. *St. Apollonia,* by Francisco de Zurbarán. The Louvre, Paris.

2-8. *The Corpse of St. Bonaventura Displayed,* by Francisco de Zurbarán. The Louvre, Paris.

2-9. *Still Life,* by Francisco de Zurbarán. The Prado, Madrid.

2-10. *St. Thomas* (detail), by Diego Velázquez. Musée des Beaux-Arts, Orléans.

2-11. *The Water Seller of Seville,* by Diego Velázquez. Wellington Museum, London.

2-12. *Old Woman Cooking Eggs* (detail), by Diego Velázquez. National Gallery of Scotland, Edinburgh.

2-13. *The Surrender of Breda* (detail), by Diego Velázquez. The Prado, Madrid. (Also called by its Spanish name, *Las Lanzas.*)

2-14. *Las Meninas,* by Diego Velázquez. The Prado, Madrid. (Also known as *The Family of Philip IV.*)

2-15. *Prince Baltasar Carlos on Horseback,* by Diego Velázquez. The Prado, Madrid.

2-16. *Garden of the Villa Medici in Rome,* by Diego Velázquez. The Prado, Madrid.

2-17. *Las Hilanderas* (detail), by Diego Velázquez. The Prado, Madrid. (In English, *The Spinners,* but originally recorded as *The Fable of Arachne.*)

2-18. *Christ as the Good Shepherd,* by Bartolomé Esteban Murillo. The Prado, Madrid.

2-19. *Boys Eating Melons and Grapes* (detail), by Bartolomé Esteban Murillo. Alte Pinakothek, Munich.

2-20. *Still Life with Salmon and Lemon,* by Luis Egidio Meléndez. The Prado, Madrid.

2-21. Doorway of the Hospicio de San Fernando, Madrid, by Pedro de Ribera. (This is the present-day Municipal Museum and Library.)

2-22. The *Transparente* Altar, Cathedral of Toledo, by Narciso Tomé. (The degree of collaboration by his father and his brothers remains problematic, and major credit is generally assigned to Narciso.)

2-23. Main Altar of the Seminary, Salamanca, by the Churriguera family.

3-39. *Calm Sea,* by Jan van de Cappelle. Wallraf-Richartz Museum, Cologne.

3-40. *Nyenrode Castle,* by Jan van der Heyden. Rijksmuseum, Amsterdam.

3-41. *Interior of the Church of St. Adolph at Assendelft,* by Pieter Saenredam. Rijksmuseum, Amsterdam.

3-42. *Interior of a Gothic Church,* by Emanuel de Witte. Rijksmuseum, Amsterdam.

3-43. *Young Couple in a Landscape,* by Frans Hals. Rijksmuseum, Amsterdam.

3-44. *Portrait of Willem Croes,* by Frans Hals. Alte Pinakothek, Munich.

3-45. *The Bohemian Girl,* by Frans Hals. The Louvre, Paris.

3-46. *The Duet,* by Hendrick Terbrugghen. The Louvre, Paris.

3-47. *Self-portrait with Saskia,* by Rembrandt van Rijn. Gemäldegalerie, Dresden.

3-48. *Stormy Landscape,* By Rembrandt van Rijn. Herzog-Anton-Ulrich Museum, Brunswick.

3-49. *Portrait of the Artist's Son Titus,* by Rembrandt van Rijn. Kunsthistorisches Museum, Vienna.

3-50. *The Night Watch* (detail), by Rembrandt van Rijn. Rijksmuseum, Amsterdam. (More accurately identified as *The Militia Company of Captain Frans Banning Cocq.*)

3-51. *The Supper at Emmaus,* by Rembrandt van Rijn. The Louvre, Paris.

3-52. *Flora* (detail), by Rembrandt van Rijn. Metropolitan Museum of Art, New York.

3-53. *Family Group,* by Rembrandt van Rijn. Herzog-Anton-Ulrich Museum, Brunswick.

3-54. Abbey Church of Rottenbuch, near Munich. (Rococo decoration added later by J. Schmuzer and F. X. Schmädle.)

3-55. Benedictine Abbey, Zwiefalten, by Johann Michael Fischer.

3-56. Church of the Fourteen Saints (Vierzehnheiligen), near Bamberg, by Balthasar Neumann.

3-57. Interior view, Church of the Fourteen Saints (Vierzehnheiligen), near Bamberg, by Balthasar Neumann.

3-58. Ballroom in the Nymphenburg Palace, near Munich, decorated by J. B. Zimmermann.

3-59. The Pagodenburg, Nymphenburg Park, by Joseph Effner.

3-60. Room in the Pagodenburg, Nymphenburg Park.

3-61. Chinese Room in the Pagodenburg, Nymphenburg Park.

3-62. The Amalienburg, Nymphenburg Park, by François de Cuvilliés.

4-1. Banqueting Hall, London, by Inigo Jones.

4-2. Hatfield House, Hertfordshire, by Robert Lyming.

4-3. St. Paul's Cathedral, London, by Sir Christopher Wren.

4-4. Library of Trinity College, Cambridge, by Sir Christopher Wren.

4-5. Senate House, Cambridge, by James Gibbs.

4-6. Radcliffe Camera, Oxford, by James Gibbs.

4-7. Prior Park, Bath, by John Wood, Sr.

4-8. Derby House, London, by Robert Adam.

4-9. *Portrait of a Woman,* by Sir Peter Lely. Carrara Academy, Bergamo.

4-10. *Portrait of Mrs. Siddons as the Tragic Muse,* by Sir Joshua Reynolds. Dulwich College Gallery, London.

4-11. *Portrait of the Misses Waldegrave,* by Sir Joshua Reynolds. National Gallery of Scotland, Edinburgh.

4-12. *Portrait of Master Hare,* by Sir Joshua Reynolds. The Louvre, Paris.

4-13. *Landscape with Cornard Village,* by Sir Thomas Gainsborough. National Gallery of Scotland, Edinburgh.

4-14. *Conversation in the Park,* by Sir Thomas Gainsborough. The Louvre, Paris.

4-15. *Portrait of Mrs. Graham,* by Sir Thomas Gainsborough. National Gallery of Scotland, Edinburgh.

4-16. *Portrait of Mrs. Siddons,* by Sir Thomas Gainsborough. National Gallery, London.

4-17. *Mary and Margaret, The Painter's Daughters,* by Sir Thomas Gainsborough. Victoria and Albert Museum, London.

4-18. *The Reverend Robert Walker Skating,* by Sir Henry Raeburn. National Gallery of Scotland, Edinburgh.

4-19. *Portrait of Miss Elizabeth Farren,* by Sir Thomas Lawrence. Metropolitan Museum of Art, New York.

4-20. *Molly Longlegs with a Jockey,* by George Stubbs. Walker Art Gallery, Liverpool.

4-21. *The Thames, near Marble Hill, Twickenham,* by Richard Wilson. National Gallery, London.

4-22. *The End of the Hunt,* by George Morland. National Gallery of Art, Washington, D.C.

4-23. *The Artist's Servants,* by William Hogarth. National Gallery, London.

4-24. *The Shrimp Girl,* by William Hogarth. National Gallery, London.

4-25. *Marriage à la Mode* (detail), Scene I, by William Hogarth. National Gallery, London.

FRANCE

INDEX

F-420

F-420